WORKBOOK IN SECOND LANGUAGE ACQUISITION

Larry Selinker / Susan Gass
University of Michigan

NEWBURY HOUSE PUBLISHERS, INC.
ROWLEY, MASSACHUSETTS 01969
ROWLEY • LONDON • TOKYO

1 9 8 4

Library of Congress Cataloging in Publication Data

Selinker, Larry, 1937–
   Workbook in second language acquisition.

   Includes bibliographical references and index.
   1. Language acquisition. 2. Language and languages--
Study and teaching. I. Gass, Susan. II. Title.
P118.S39   1984   418'.007   84-4913
ISBN 0-88377-435-6

We dedicate this book to
Michael, Aaron, Seth, and Ethan

NEWBURY HOUSE PUBLISHERS, INC.

Language Science
Language Teaching
Language Learning

ROWLEY, MASSACHUSETTS 01969
ROWLEY • LONDON • TOKYO

First printing: June 1984

Printed in the U.S.A.   5   4   3   2   1

FOREWORD

In 1972, Larry Selinker, in his paper, "Interlanguage," discussed the "psychologically-relevant data of second-language learning" and issued a call for researchers to seek out this sort of data. Since that beginning in 1972, of course, a great many studies in second-language acquisition (SLA) have been done, and a significant body of data has been gathered together. Given this history, it is appropriate that, in 1984, Larry Selinker should join with Susan Gass in calling again for a focus on data in our field—but this time, in the teaching of courses in SLA.

Courses in SLA are now routinely taught in graduate programs for the training of ESL teachers, and a number of texts have been written for such courses—texts which summarize for the neophyte teacher the "state of the art" in SLA research. But up to this point, there has been no text which provided the opportunity for teachers-in-training to work with structured data themselves: to do more than simply read summaries of the state of the art or published studies in SLA, but rather to exercise their own insights and creativity in analyzing bits of language produced by second-language learners. As Selinker and Gass argue in the introduction to this workbook, it is only by working firsthand with the data that students new to this field really come to understand the complexity of the issues involved in SLA.

This workbook will make it possible for instructors to systematically change the way that courses in SLA are taught. First, I think courses in SLA will be more interesting for the inclusion of problems such as those in this workbook. Playing with data can be fun, and giving students the opportunity to try their own hands at data analysis and interpretation can only make SLA courses more involving and enjoyable for students, who are sometimes suspicious of science and research.

Second, this workbook will immediately involve teacher-trainees in the *process* of SLA research, instead of presenting them with apparently finished *products* in the form of published papers. It has been my impression in teaching courses in SLA that teacher-trainees are often overly impressed by research articles in print, the final product of the research process. They are often too likely to accept the conclusions of the author as final, without understanding the process of research which led to those conclusions. They need to learn firsthand that research results are part of a process which is not an occult mystery but rather a process which they themselves may participate in and contribute to. This workbook should help immensely in demythologizing research. I would expect that students who have worked with the language samples in this workbook will become teachers who see that they too can contribute to the development of this field to at least some degree—that research is not simply to be left to the experts or to published papers.

At the same time that this workbook should help to dispel the often-undeserved magic of "resarch-in-print," it should also help to make students aware of the complexities involved in this sort of research. SLA data are often messy. The answer is not always immediately apparent—or even there. More than one interpretation of the data is usually not only possible, but necessary. It is only by working with SLA data oneself that one really comes to appreciate these truths—and once one does appreciate them, one is less likely to accept the more simplistic theories of SLA which may be proposed in the literature from time to time. I would expect students who have worked with data such as those presented in this workbook to be more critical consumers of research.

Finally, the workbook should encourage greater breadth in SLA courses, including, as it does, a nice range of areas of SLA: discourse as well as morphological data, "specific-purposes" acquisition as well as syntactic data. In addition, in the questions following each data set, there has been an attempt to involve students in the consideration of many of the current issues in the field. This breadth and relevance should help make the workbook more usable in the SLA class and discourage too narrow a focus on the part of the instructor and the trainees.

The field of SLA is built upon data, in the last analysis. Theories and models of the acquisition process are important, but they must ultimately rest upon a solid foundation of observable and verifiable facts about the language produced by second-language learners. By encouraging teacher-trainees and teaching researchers to regularly return to the data upon which the theoretical edifices of SLA rest, this workbook should make an important contribution, not simply to the SLA classroom, but in some measure to the entire field of SLA.

University of Minnesota   Elaine Tarone
January 1984

CONTENTS

"*To my data, right or wrong.*"

Drawing by Levin; © 1984—The New Yorker Magazine, Inc.

INTRODUCTION

As a result of teaching courses over the years in second language acquisition (SLA), we have come to the realization that without some "hands-on" experience with actual second language data, students in these courses have an incomplete understanding of the theoretical principles which we are trying to teach. Without actually seeing exemplars of the kinds of interlanguages (ILs) learners do and do not produce, there seems to be a barrier to the comprehension of the principles underlying these ILs. However, we have also found that, generally speaking, these same students have difficulty handling the complexities of raw data as they occur in nonnative speaker speech. Thus, partial organization of the data presented seems to be necessary. As a result, this workbook represents a compromise in that learner data are presented in an organized fashion to illustrate particular principles, with complexities eliminated when they do not contribute to an understanding of the point at issue in each problem. For this reason, data appearing here should *not* be cited directly without verification of their accuracy from original sources. We have further found that problems such as the ones presented in this workbook are important in SLA courses and regularly rate high on student evaluations; students have commented that the problems are "useful as working tools," particularly because they "force you to do something yourself, rather than simply learning what someone else says"; that they help the student see the data "from the learner's viewpoint, rather than my own NL viewpoint"; that after doing a fairly large number, "I feel like I can analyze data now"; that the problems can and often do lead to interesting class discussion "looking at the concepts in a new way."

There is another facet about teaching SLA that has motivated the form of the materials here. We find that our subject matter is one about which *everyone* seems to have an opinion. This affects our teaching in numerous ways. One way involves the student who perceives learner behavior as a mirror image of language teaching. That is, this student attempts to "explain" all IL forms on the basis of language instruction. Another way involves the student who perceives L2 behavior as a mirror image of the L1. This student thus attempts to "explain" IL forms solely on the basis of "interference" from the learner's native language. Clearly, what has to be recognized is that while the above-mentioned perceptions exist as possible explanations of IL facts, they are in the majority of cases overly simplistic in accounting for the appearance of IL forms.

This leads to a general problem. Students often appear compelled to look for *the* answer in terms of simple explanations to a given set of IL data. Researchers, after many years of experience, learn that this search for unique explanations is fraught with difficulty. How does one aid students in SLA courses to deal adequately with complexities of data? We have tried to deal with this question in this workbook by providing students with a basis for creating and evaluating the plausibility of explanations for L2 data. In using this workbook, thus, we think that it is important that students *work through problems from beginning to end.* Because the information in a problem is often cumulative, we suggest that teachers encourage students to do Part I of a problem fully before looking at Part II, etc.

We have several criteria for inclusion of the materials that appear here. First, we want to cover a wide range of issues that have been discussed in the SLA literature. Second, we want to include a variety of choices of topics so that individual teachers can focus on different aspects of SLA, according to their own preferences. Third, we want to present as wide a range of ILs as possible, bearing in mind the paucity of non-English-based IL data in the literature. Fourth, we want to have problems which are doable in the sense that students can feel a sense of accomplishment in dealing with each particular data set, our goal being that students *can* produce a possible analysis, keeping in mind that there is not necessarily a unique solution for each problem.

An important feature of this workbook is the gradation of questions within problems. We include questions for selected data sets which are more difficult than questions which appear earlier in the data problems. These more difficult ones are starred (*) for easy recognition. (We thank Jacquelyn Schachter for this suggestion.) A double star (**) implies even greater difficulty. Our experience is that these starred questions enable more advanced students to go beyond the original data, learning to incorporate more and greater complexities of L2 data into their analyses. This feature allows this workbook to be used not only for introductory courses in SLA but also for more advanced courses, including courses primarily devoted to data analysis. The reader will also note that throughout the workbook, there are questions which suggest that additional data need to be gathered in order to decide on the correctness of an analysis. Thus, students are provided with a jumping-off point for gathering original data. It is also important to note that the ordering of data within a problem does not imply developmental order unless specifically specified.

The basic organizing principle of this workbook is language categories, with a final section on methodology and research design. Important concepts in SLA such as language transfer, fossilization, and acquisition order have not been neglected. Rather, they are a primary focus of the problems within each section. There is no intention to order the problems in any way within a section, although to make a more coherent whole and to allow students to see interconnections of IL data, cross referencing is often provided within a section and across sections. Section 1 covers problems in Morphology, Section 2 Lexicon, Section 3 Phonology, Section 4 Syntax/Semantics, Section 5 Spoken and Written Discourse, Section 6 Foreigner Talk Discourse, Section 7 Specific Purpose Acquisition, and Section 8 Methodology and Research Design.

The problems themselves are placed into sections for ease of presentation; where there is overlap in terms of categories, we intend no implicit theoretical statement for selecting one category over another. The introductory remarks for each section are intended to introduce students to concepts which are important for an understanding of the problems.

There are three appendixes. In order to present more fieldlike conditions for advanced students, in Appendix I we present fuller data sets to selected problems. These longer data sets may be used for term projects, should the instructor wish. In Appendix II we acknowledge the references for particular data sets, and in Appendix III we provide an index of all the interlanguages used in this workbook.

We wrestled with the idea of providing an answer guide along with this workbook. There are pros and cons to this issue. We finally decided to provide such a guide, which is intended to serve as a general orientation to the problems. It is our strong feeling that part of the educational value to doing problems in SLA courses is to instruct students on the nature of argumentation based on IL data. Our guide therefore provides possible solutions and is not intended to imply that there is a unique solution for any of the problems.

The problems in this workbook have been drawn from a variety of sources: published literature, colleagues' gracious sharing of research materials, and our own research materials. (See Appendix II for specific acknowledgment for the source of each problem used.)

We thank the following for their serious encouragement for this project: Ellen Adiv, Janusz Arabski, Josh Ard, Lyle Bachman, Bruce Barkman, Guillermo Bartelt, Charlotte Basham, Ed Beniak, Ellen Broselow, Moira Chimombo, Andrew Cohen, Alan Davies, Raphel Gefen, Cindy Greenberg, Edith Hanania, Lynne Hansen, Birgit Harley, Einar Haugen, Laura Heilenman, Liet Hellwig, Thom Huebner, Georgette Ioup, Peter Jordens, Deborah Keller-Cohen, Eric Kellerman, James Lantolf, Diane Larsen-Freeman, Patsy Lightbown, Colette Noyau, Elite Olshtain, Cathy Pettinari, Dennis Preston, Pat Rounds, Robert Ramsey, John Schumann, Herb Seliger, Michael Sharwood Smith, Amy Sheldon, Elaine Tarone, Russ Tomlin, Jan Ulijn, Benji Wald, Joel Walters, Mari Wesche, Henning Wode, and Helmut Zobl. We are also extremely grateful to all those who have contributed data (see Appendix II).

We would like to single out a number of people for their special contribution to this workbook. We thank Elizabeth Lantz of Newbury House for her patience and astute comments from the inception of this project to its completion. The comments we received from Russ Tomlin proved to be extremely helpful in our revising of the manuscript. Because of his comments, this version is a greatly improved one. Josh Ard has provided serious intellectual input and personal encouragement throughout all phases of this project. Rosemary Tackabery and Judy Sudak deserve special mention for their assistsance in the preparation of the manuscript. Finally, and in some sense most importantly, we wish to thank our students. They have helped us to deal seriously with second language data.

Like other scholars we have built on the work of our predecessors. We have looked at numerous workbooks in linguistics and related and unrelated fields; we particularly owe much to the works by Nida (1946), Gleason (1955), and Halle and Clements (1983) in terms of format and general organizational principles.

We envision that this workbook will be used primarily in SLA courses, at the introductory level. It can also be used in other courses with second language components, for example, courses in ESL theory and/or methodology. In both cases, we intend the materials to accompany readings and/or textbooks selected by the instructor. We would like to further suggest that this workbook could serve as the central text for laboratory courses or seminars devoted exclusively to the analysis of second language data.

ABBREVIATIONS

IL	Interlanguage	FTD	Foreigner talk discourse
NL	Native language	SVO	Subject-verb-object
TL	Target language	SOV	Subject-object-verb
NNS	Nonnative speaker	L2	Second language
NS	Native speaker	SLA	Second language acquisition

SECTION 1

Morphology

In this section we present 10 problems on IL morphology. The following concepts in the field of second language acquisition are relevant to the problems and should help in understanding the issues raised:

1. Developmental progression
2. Unanalyzed units
3. Obligatory context
4. Individual differences
5. Order of acquisition

Developmental progression refers to changes over time in a learner's L2 grammar.

Unanalyzed units are those units which learners consider a single unit but which are actually comprised of more than one unit in terms of the target language.

Obligatory context is a means for considering if a particular structure has or has not been acquired. It refers to whether or not a particular form is or is not used when the standard language requires its use.

The concept of *individual differences* among learners is important in analyzing L2 grouped data. It is also necessary to bear in mind that there are many ways people go about learning a second language, so that the study of individual approaches to the learning task is as important as the study of what is common to all L2 learners.

Order of acquisition involves the claim that some units/forms are acquired before others and that the researcher can determine that order. Most of the research in this area has been carried out on IL morphology.

PROBLEM 1.1

Native Language: Polish
Target Language: English
Background Information: High school and university students
Data Source: Student compositions on the topic: "Why I wouldn't like to get married before I finish my studies."

Part I

Data

1. I will been 19 years. It's a very beautiful times in my life. I am going to **studying**.
2. The married and **studing**—a very hard things.
3. What it been when I will not **studying**.
4. No, I will not **getting** married, because I am **going** to **working** and **studying**. I will **adding** the married I will been verry difficult and I not.
5. The married a very serious things. I am afraid the married I am must **knowing**. He's **loveing** me and I must **loving** him.
6. I must **learning** a very things in the more married.
7. It's a more thing serious thing and I will not to **getting** married if I will been 25 years.

Questions

1. Focus on the words in boldface. Describe the verbal morphology system that these learners are using.

2. How does the IL system of these learners differ from the standard English system?

Part II

Data

1. After a graduation I wouldn't get married. Because I wount to go to university and I wount to do something on my country and the other people.
2. I'm going to do a lot of things. Married it's a hard thing.
3. When I'll graduation, I wouldn't to get married, because I want to go to university.
4. Later I want to do on my country and a lot of things for other people.
5. Married is very difficult thing.
6. I think that people wouldn't get married right after graduation.
7. I think that people 18 years old are too young for that. I think that first we must finish our learn and then get married.
8. But we can get married when we are studying or working.
9. We can get married when we are 24—26 years old.
10. I wouldn't get married after graduation. I think that 18 years is too young age for this.
11. I think first we must be educate and then to get married.
12. This days medium educate doesn't give anything, one must first finish study or a school after high school.

13. I think that one can get married while he is studying.
14. I thing that men 18 years old is too young to get married. The marriage won't be long and woman will be unhappy.
15. Youth is very short and one must make use for this.

Questions

3. Focus on the verbs in these data. Describe the verbal morphology system these learners are using.

4. If you treated the term *get married* as an unanalyzed unit (see composition topic, page 00), would this change your analysis, and if so, how?

*5. Do you think these learners are more or less advanced than the learners of Part I? On what do you base this conclusion?

*6. What, if any, conclusions can you draw about the acquisition of morphology by L2 learners? You might in addition want to do Problem 2.1 and compare your conclusions drawn from that problem with those drawn from this problem.

PROBLEM 1.2

Native Language: Arabic
Target Language: English
Background Information: Three adult subjects, intermediate to advanced
Data Source: Compositions and conversations

Data

1. There are also **two deserts**.
2. I bought **a couple of towel**.
3. So, when I like to park my car, there is no place to put it, and **how many ticket** I took.
4. There is **many kind of way** you make baklawa.
5. **The streets** run from east to west, **the avenues** from north to south.
6. I go to university **four days** a week.
7. Just **a few month** he will finish from his studies.
8. Egypt shares **its boundaries** with the Mediterranean.
9. There is **a lot of mosquito**.
10. **Many people** have **ideas** about Jeddah and other cities located in Saudi Arabia.
11. When he complete **nine month**.
12. He can spend **100 years** here in America.
13. There are about **one and half-million inhabitant** in Jeddah.
14. How **many month or years** have been in his mind?
15. There are **many tents—and goats** running around.
16. There are **two mountains**.
17. How **many hour**?
18. There are more than **200,000 telephone lines**.
19. Every country had **three or four kind of bread**.

Questions

1. Focus on the phrases in boldface and categorize the data according to "correct" English-like vs. non-English-like patterns of plural usage. Continue the format illustrated below:

English-like	*Non-English-like*
two deserts	a couple of towel
⋮	⋮

2. What IL generalization(s) might account for this particular pattern of usage?

*3. What further data would you like from these learners to test your hypothesis?

5

PROBLEM 1.3

Native Language: Mexican Spanish
Target Language: English
Background Information: Adult male
Data Source: Tape-recorded spontaneous speech

Part I

Data

Following are examples of this subject's use of negatives:

1. No write.
2. No like it.
3. I me no speaka too much Englee, eh?
4. Me no like stay in the house.
5. No es correct.
6. I no like tortilla.
7. You no go Calexico?
8. My brother no go to school.
9. No, ya no work.
10. Me no comin.
11. No in town.
12. No cheese.
13. No now.
14. No American.
15. Ye operation ya no good.
16. No money.
17. Maybe no good for me.

Questions

1. Describe this learner's knowledge of English negation.

2. At this same time, this nonnative speaker produced many examples of *I don't know.* Does this alter your hypothesis about the pattern described in question 1? If so, how?

Part II

Data

During the same taping session, this speaker also produced the following utterances:

1. Not too much.
2. Not too mucha.
3. No, not it.
4. Not eate sugar.
5. Not too good.

Of the 85 examples of negatives which this speaker produced, approximately 82 percent were of the type given in Part I while 18 percent were of the type given in Part II.

Questions

3. What explanations can you come up with to account for the difference?

4. What additional data might you have liked to elicit from this speaker to aid in determining which of the possible explanations proposed in question 3 are plausible and which are not?

*5. What would you expect his IL to be like at a later point in time?

*6. If you were to learn that this person was 68 years old and had been living in the United States for 31 years at the time of this taping session, would your answer to question 5 be any different? How?

Native Language: Arabic
Target Language: English
Background Information: Beginner (no formal English instruction)
Data Source: Spontaneous utterances

Data[1]

Time 1
No (imperative)[2]
No English (I can't speak English)

Time 2
No (answer to question)
I can't speak English
My husband not here
Not raining

Time 3
No (answer to question)
I can't speak English
My husband not here

My husband not home
Don't touch
Don't touch it

Time 4
My husband not here
Hani not sleeping
I can't speak English
No, I can't understand
I don't know
Don't eat
No, this is . . . (answer to question)

Questions

1. What is the progression from the first time period to the fourth in terms of this learner's development of English negation? Give specifics about her knowledge at each time period.

2. There is some evidence that *can't* and *don't* are being used as unanalyzed units. What evidence can you bring to bear to support this conclusion?

3. Focus on time 4. Do *can't* and *don't* still seem to be unanalyzed units? Justify your response.

---

[1]Assume that the lack of certain forms in early stages represents subject's inability to produce them. They are not accidental gaps.
[2]Intended meanings are discernible from context.

*4. Compare your results on this problem with those of Problem 1.3, where a different NL is involved. What does this comparison suggest about negation across ILs?

Native Language: Spanish
Target Language: English
Background Information: Child, age 11, in the United States since age 7
Data Source: Spontaneous utterances

=== Part I ===

Data[1]

1. When I do something they don't hit me. (When I do something wrong they don't hit me.)
2. The mother doesn't want to take him away. (His mother didn't want to take him away.)
3. He doesn't hear 'cause he was already dead. (He didn't hear because he had already died.)
4. He don't buy us nothing. (He never buys us anything.)
5. She don't help her nothing, muy floja. (She never helps her; she's real lazy.)
6. They still doesn't know 'cause they work in another country. (They hadn't found out yet because they were working in another country.)

Questions

1. What systematic distinction does this learner make between her use of *don't* and *doesn't*?

2. What further data would you want to elicit from this subject in order to determine the generalizability of your analysis?

=== Part II ===

Data

I always **do** the dishes and I hate it. When she **do** the . . . food she **say** to me, if you **don't** help me you **don't** eat . . . and she **do** it.

Questions

3. Do these data support or refute the conclusions you came up with in Part I?

---

[1]The material in parentheses gives the sense of the utterances in a standard English form. This sense is discernible from context.

4. What does this learner know about forming third person singular present tense verb forms?

*5. Consider the following utterance also produced by this learner: "She ask me if I **did** it and I say I **did**." Does this alter your analysis in any way? If so, how?

Native Language: Arabic
Target Language: English
Background Information: Beginner (no formal English instruction)
Data Source: Spontaneous utterances

Data[1]

1. He's sleeping.
2. She's sleeping.
3. It's raining.
4. He's eating.
5. Hani's sleeping.
6. The dog eating. (The dog is eating.)
7. Hani watch TV. (Hani is watching TV.)
8. Watch TV. (He is watching TV.)
9. Read the paper. (He is reading the paper.)
10. Drink the coffee. (He is drinking coffee.)

Questions

1. From these data one could hypothesize that the learner is using an IL rule which restricts the occurrence of V-ing to sentence final position. What other possible analysis is there to account for the variation in her correct and incorrect use of the English progressive?

*2. What additional data would you want to elicit to determine the correctness of your conclusion versus the one presented in question 1?

---

[1]The material in parentheses gives the sense of the utterances in standard English form. This sense is discernible from context.   **13**

PROBLEM 1.7

Native Language: Arabic
Target Language: English
Background Information: Three subjects, intermediate to advanced
Data Source: Compositions and conversations

Part I

Data

1. You can find it **from Morocco til Saudi Arabia**.
2. There is many kind **of way** you make baklawa.
3. It's some kind **of different**.
4. I don't like to buy a car **from Ann Arbor**.
5. **Since long time**, I'm buying B.F. Goodrich.
6. He finished his studies **before one month**.
7. He will finish **from his studies**.
8. They are many kinds of reptiles which live **at this planet**.
9. I never help my mom **in the housework**.
10. Egypt shares its boundaries with the Mediterranean Sea on the north, **the Red Sea from the east**.

Questions

1. Focus on the phrases in boldface. Describe the use of prepositions in these data.

2. How does the description of the data for Part I differ from a description of standard English?

Part II

Data

1. We used to pronounce everything **British English**.
2. It doesn't give me problems **future**.
3. He's working **his thesis** now.
4. If I come early, I will register **fall**.
5. The people are outside **this time**.
6. About 20 kilometer out **Jeddah**.
7. I'll wait **you**.

Questions

3. Consider the words and phrases in boldface in Part II. Describe the IL generalizations in these data relating your description to the use of prepositions in English.

15

*4. Compare the IL generalization(s) you have created for Part II with those of Part I in terms of preposition usage.

======= Part III =======

Data

1. Since I came **to the United States**.
2. I have lived **in downtown Ann Arbor**.
3. There are 25 counties **in Egypt**.
4. You might think you are **in Dallas**.
5. I have noticed there are many **of them**.
6. They are genius **in this area**.
7. I will go speak nice **to him**.
8. Beginning **from 1:30 a.m. until 2:00 a.m.**

Questions

*5. Describe what the subjects seem to know about prepositions in these data.

**6. Do the above data alter the IL generalizations of Parts I and II? If so, how?

**7. What additional data might you like to have from these learners?

PROBLEM 1.8

Native Language: English
Target Language: French
Background Information: Second year immersion, ages 7-1/2
Data Source: Free conversation, picture description and story-telling

Part I

Data

Interlanguage

Standard French

1. Elle fait   le   peinture avec le   confiture
   she makes the painting with the jam
             m.   f.   m.   f.

   Elle met de la   confiture sur le   pain
   she puts of the jam   on   the bread

   Intended Meaning[1]: She's putting jam on the bread

2. le   fille
   the girl
   m.   f.

   la   fille
   the (f.)

   Intended Meaning: the girl

3. la   garçon
   the boy
   f.   m.

   le   garçon
   the (m.)

   Intended Meaning: the boy

4. Il   va   sur mon lit
   he goes on   my   bed
              m.   m.

   il va   sur mon lit

   Intended Meaning: He goes on my bed

5. Il   dort   en bas   de ma lit
   he sleeps in   bottom of my bed
                       f.   m.

   il dort par terre   près de mon lit
           on the ground near of my   bed
                                m.   m.

   Intended Meaning: He sleeps on the floor

6. Mon maman et   moi et   tous   mon   soeurs et
   my   mother and me and all   my   sisters and
   m.   m.pl.   m.sg.   pl.

   Ma maman et   moi et   toutes mes soeurs
   my mother and me and all   my   sisters

   tous   mes   frères
   all   my   brothers
   m.pl. m.pl. pl.

   et tous mes frères

   Intended Meaning: My mother and I and all my sisters and all my brothers

Questions

1. One could argue that gender assignment in ILs is at times random. Does this appear to be the case in these data?

---

[1]Discernible from context.

2. If not, what is the IL generalization that these learners are making about gender in French? How could this be tested?

=========== **Part II** ===========

Data

Marking on third person pronouns

	Obligatory context masculine % correct	*Obligatory context feminine % correct*
Time 1	100	33
Time 2	100	86

Questions

2. Does the information presented above change the conclusions which you drew from Part I? If so, how?

=========== **Part III** ===========

Data

Individual learners' performance

	obligatory/masculine (% corr.)		*obligatory/feminine (% corr.)*	
Child	*Time 1*	*Time 2*	*Time 1*	*Time 2*
1	100	100	0	75
2	—[1]	90	10	100
3	100	100	0	100
4	100	100	0	90
5	100	100	0	95
6	—	100	60	60
7	—	100	75	60
8	—	100	40	80
9	100	100	100	90
10	100	100	100	100

[1]Scores were not included when there were fewer than five obligatory contexts.

Questions

3. Consider the individual differences of these children. Describe the pattern you find individual by individual. Does looking at individuals alter any generalizations you may have made thus far?

*4. What limitations are there to looking at percentage differences among individuals?

*5. In French all nouns are either masculine or feminine. Natural gender is used when appropriate. Consider the data in Parts I and II from the point of view of contrastive analysis. Are these results predictable on the basis of an NL-TL comparison? Why, or why not?

Native Language: Spanish
Target Language: English
Background Information: Preadolescents, born in Mexico, living in United States
Data Source: Responses to a picture story from a standard proficiency test

Data

Below are "correct" responses to standardized test items.
1. He **wants** to eat some food.
2. The dog **ate** the food.
3. The king **would have eaten** it.
4. It **fell**.

The English feature being tested in each case is:
1. Third singular -s with "want"
2. Past tense of "eat"
3. Pluperfect conditional, i.e., existence and form of auxiliary, perfect form of auxiliary, past participle
4. past tense of "fall"

Below are responses to these test items by five ESL learners.

A. 1. he wants to eat.
   2. the dog ate it.
   3. the king would eat it.
   4. it fell.
B. 1. he want the food.
   2. the dog ate. . . .
   3. the king eat. . . .
   4. they fall.
C. 1. he wants to get some food.
   2. the dog ate it.

3. the king would have ate it.
4. it fell.
D. 1. he want. . . .
   2. the dog eat. . . .
   3. the king will eat. . . .
   4. it fall.
E. 1. he wanna eat. . . .
   2. the dog eat—ate it.
   3. he would eat it.
   4. it fall.

Questions

1. Who appears to be the most advanced learner and why?

2. Who appears to be the least advanced learner and why?

3. What generalization can be made about the order of acquisition for learning these constructions? In answering this, it may be helpful to lay out the data for each speaker in a matrix, as below:

Feature tested

Subject	F_1	F_2	F_3	F_4	F_5
A					
B					
C					
D					
E					

*4. Tests of this type are designed primarily to elicit spontaneous utterances in a controlled setting. What limitations are there in doing order of acquisition analysis based on data of this sort?

Native Language: Spanish
Target Language: English
Background Information: Adult immigrant in the United States
Data Source: Spontaneous speech

Data

Week 1
Don't remember how you say it.
We don't know how automobile.
I don't understand.
I don't have time to go to college.

Week 3
I don't have the car.
I no understand.
No remember.
No understand that.
No have pronunciation.
No is mine.
Because no gain for the year.

Week 7
I no understand.
I no understand this question.
I no make, no can repeat the (oración),[1] no?
I don't can explain.

Week 11
I don't talk English.
I don't can more.
I don't understand this name.
I no like my coffee.
I no can explain this.
You no will come here this vacation?

Week 17
I don't understand.
I don't have a woman.
I no remember.
In my country no haves too much friends.

No like more, thank you.
No talk to him.

Week 21
I no like this summer.
Maybe no like this state.
I no have friend.
I no have application.
No is problem.
I no can walk.

Week 27
No eat meat.
I don't saw.
People don't can pass the jungle.
No can make nothing.
No put sick.
Maybe she no live more.

Week 33
I don't understand this question.
I don't remember this name.
I no speak English very nice, no?
I no remember this name.
This isn't a supper, is a lunch.
No is good place.

Week 35
I don't care.
I don't understand.
No have sister.
I no eat nothing.
No drink nothing.
I don't can explain this picture.

Questions

1. Describe the subject's negative structures as they develop over time.

---

[1] Word only faintly heard, but guessable

2. Describe his auxiliary structures (*do, is,* modal words) as they develop over time.

3. If you consider *don't* as a formulaic expression, what overall analysis can you provide for this learner's development of negation?

*4. Describe the supplementary data in Appendix I. Note that elicited data are also provided. Are the elicited data different from the spontaneous speech data? If so, how do you justify this difference?

SECTION 2

Lexicon

Among the key concepts covered in the eight problems in this section are:

1. (Over)generalization
2. Language transfer (transferability)
3. Bidirectionality

Generalizations are frequently made of target material. For example, in child language acquisition there are numerous examples of children producing *comed*, which is an overextension of the regular past tense form.

Language transfer most commonly refers to the use of NL information (phonological, grammatical, organizational, etc.) in the acquisition of a second language.

Bidirectionality concerns language transfer effects that work equally in two directions, e.g., French speakers learning English vs. English speakers learning French.

PROBLEM 2.1

Native Languages: Mixed
Target Language: English
Background Information: Intermediate level students in an intensive course
Data Source: Part I, free conversation; Part II, student compositions; Part III, student compositions

Part I

Data

1. I had one **discuss** with my brother.
2. You have a business **relation**. (relationship)[1]
3. You get happy very **easy**.
4. There will be two **child**.
5. You say he's a **science**.
6. We have to think about Franklin, the **science**.
7. She has a good chance to **life**.
8. Maybe they don't finish their **educated**.

Questions

1. How do the forms in boldface differ from standard English usage?

2. Is there a consistent predictable relationship between these IL forms and standard usage?

Part II

Data

1. Actually such **behaves** lead mostly to misunderstanding.
2. The people give presents to **they** friend and their family.
3. Some people didn't **belief** this was a better way.
4. No matter how **differ** in age between us.
5. **Differ** from other parents in my country, they never told us what we must study.
6. Taught me how to choose the more **advantages** values.
7. This is a strange but **interest** continent.
8. The most **advantage** way.

Questions

3. Focus on the words in boldface in each sentence. Work out an IL generalization which might account for these forms. Give your reasons for postulating this generalization.

[1]Intended meaning discernible from context.

4. Compare the generalization(s) you have created for these written IL data with what you have created for the oral data in Part I of this problem.

===== **Part III** =====

Data

1. Soccer is the most common **sporting**.
2. America refused continual **supported** our military request.
3. When he was 7 years old, he went **schooling**.
4. About two hours driving **eastern** from Bangkok.
5. After finished my college **studied**, I went to my country.
6. Doctors have the right to **removed** it from him.
7. There is a night for **asleep**.
8. Moreover it may lead to **conflicting**.
9. I am not going to get married when I will **graduation** the school.

Questions

5. Work out an IL generalization that might account for the forms in boldface. Give your reasons for postulating this generalization.

*6. Does this new information change the generalization(s) you came up with in Part II? If so, how?

*7. Given the data presented in Parts I, II, and III of this problem, what strategy/strategies have these learners come up with regarding lexical use?

*8. What additional information, if any, would you like to have from these learners to test your hypothesis?

Native Language: English
Target Language: French
Background Information: Second year immersion, ages 7-1/2
Data Source: Free conversation, picture description and story-telling

Information about French: The forms appearing in boldface type in the IL are all infinitives. In French, verbs agree in person and number with the subject. Past tense is conjugated with an auxiliary (either *avoir* "to have" or *être* "to be") plus the past participle of the verb. When *être* is used, the past participle agrees in gender with the subject.

Data

Interlanguage	*Standard French*

1. Quand on **faire** "wouf" il entend
    when one to do wouf   he hears

    Intended Meaning[1]: When we go "wouf" he hears

    Quand on fait   "wouf" il entend
    3p.sg.

2. Mon maman et mon papa **aller** à Glendon
    My mom   and my dad to go to Glendon

    Intended Meaning: My Mom and Dad go to Glendon

    Ma maman et mon papa vont à Glendon
    3p.pl.

3. Le fille **mettre** du   confiture sur le pain
    The girl to put some jam   on the bread
    (m.)

    Intended Meaning: The girl puts jam on the bread

    La fille met   de la confiture sur le pain
    3rd.sg.

4. L'autre   fois je **aller** camping
    The other time I to go camping

    Intended Meaning: The other day I went camping

    L'autre jour je suis allé faire du camping.
    day   am gone to do some

5. Le garçon a **sortir** de l' eau
    The boy   has to go from the water

    Intended Meaning: The boy went out of the water

    Le garçon est sorti de l'eau
    is   gone

Questions

1. Based on the above data, how would you characterize these learners' knowledge of the French verbal system?

Information about French: ne pas is the negative form of the verb. *Ne* is placed before the verb and *pas* after. Je n'ai pas
                  I not have not
                  "I don't have"
In the examples *est* is the third person singular of the verb to be.

---

[1]Discernible from context.

2. Consider the following examples. What general strategy do these additional examples suggest?

Interlanguage	Standard French	Intended Meaning
A. **ne pas** loin **n'est pas** loin	pas trop loin	not too far
B. Il **n'est pas** neige	Il ne neige pas	It's not snowing

3. Consider the following exchanges:

		Interlanguage	Standard French	Intended Meaning
A.	*Q:*	Ici, qu'est-ce qu'il fait?		Here, what is he doing?
	R:	Nager to swim	Il nage he swims	Swimming
B.	*Q:*	Est-ce que tu préfères les chiens ou les chats?		Do you prefer dogs or cats?
	R:	Chats cats	les chats the cats	cats

Focus on the responses. Could you make an argument for language transfer?

*4. How does your response in question 3 relate to your analysis of those utterances in 1 to 5 above?

*5. What additional data would you want to elicit to determine what strategies underlie the production of the responses in question 3?

PROBLEM 2.3

Native Language: Arabic
Target Language: English
Background Information: Three subjects, intermediate to advanced
Data Source: Compositions and conversations

Part I

Data

1. You eat a cabbage roll **one time**.
2. I need my hair to be **tall**.
3. I hope to become **bigger** than this age.
4. **Close** the television.
5. And imagine that kind of people **graduate** every night from the bars.
6. You have hard time **to collecting** your money.
7. So, when I like to park my car, there is no place to **put it**, and **how many ticket I took**.
8. I did not **find my money in the street**.
9. This "sambousa" is not sweet or **pastry**. It's main course.
10. If I will not follow from **first**, I will not understand.
11. If you **appreciate** your money, you won't buy American car.
12. If you appreciate your money, you won't buy American car. You'll pay **expensive**.

Questions

1. Describe what you see these students doing in terms of word meaning. (This should be done sentence by sentence.)

2. Provide TL interpretations of the above sentences. (This should be done sentence by sentence.)

3. State any IL generalizations which might account for the above data and justify them. What general strategy have these learners adopted in the acquisition of English word meaning?

Data

The following are the intended meanings of the sentences in Part I.[1]

1. You ate a cabbage roll once.
2. I want my hair to be long.
3. I am looking forward to the day when my children will be older.
4. Turn off the television.
5. And imagine that kind of people will leave the bar every night.
6. You have a hard time earning your money.
7. Because there are not enough parking spaces, I get a lot of tickets.
8. Money doesn't grow on trees.
9. This "sambousa" is not a dessert. It's a main course.
10. If I don't follow the lectures from the beginning, I won't understand.
11. and 12.   If you value your money, you won't buy an American car. You will pay a lot of money . . . if you do.

Questions

4. Compare your interpretations from Part I with the intended meanings above. Describe differences if they exist. What do these differences suggest about NS biases in interpretation?

*5. Do the results of your comparison affect or change your previous IL generalizations? If so, how and why?

*6. What additional data would you like to elicit from these students and why?

[1]Discerned from playback sessions in the native language.

PROBLEM 2.4

Native Language: English
Target Language: French
Background Information: Second year immersion program, ages 7-1/2
Data Source: Free conversation, picture description, story-telling

Part I

Data

Interlanguage

1. Elle **marche** les chats
    she walks   the cats

    Intended Meaning[1]: She's walking the cats

2. **des temps**
    of the times

    Intended Meaning: sometimes

3. Il **est** trois ans
    he is 3   years

    Intended Meaning: He's three years old

4. Il **regarde comme** six ans
    he looks   like   six years

    Intended Meaning: He looks six years old

5. Ca **regarde** très drôle
    that looks   very funny

    Intended Meaning: It looks very funny

6. Ses cheveux **looks comme** un garçon
    Her hair   looks like   a   boy

    Intended Meaning: Her hair looks like a boy's

7. Je dois de **spell** mon nom pour toi
    I   must of spell my   name for you

    Intended Meaning: I have to spell my name for you

8. Je vais manger des   pour souper
    I go to eat some for   supper

    Intended Meaning: I'm going to eat some for supper

Standard French

Elle fait faire   une promenade aux   chats
she makes to do a   walk   to the cats
        (causative)

a. parfois
b. quelquefois
c. des fois

Il a   trois ans
    has

Il a   l'air   de six ans
he has the air of

Ca   semble très drôle
that seems

a. Ses cheveux semblent être   ceux d'un garçon
                       seem   to be those of a boy

b. Ses cheveux ressemblent à ceux d'un garçon
                      resemble   to

a. Je dois épeler   mon nom pour toi
              to spell

b. Je dois t'épeler   mon nom
              to spell you

Je vais en   manger pour souper
I go   some to eat

Questions

1. What linguistic information do these learners seem to be transferring in each instance?

---

[1]Discernible from context.

Data

Interlanguage	*Standard French*

1. Le chien **a mangé les.**
   the dog has eaten them

   Le chien les a mangés
   the dog them has eaten

   Intended Meaning[1]: The dog ate them

2. Il **veut les** encore
   he wants them still

   Il les veut encore

   Intended Meaning: He still wants them

3. des **drôles films**
   some funny movies

   des films drôles

   Intended Meaning: some funny movies

4. Je aller le **français camp**
   I to go the French camp

   Je vais aller au camp français
   I go to go to the camp French

   Intended Meaning: I'm going to go to a French camp

5. Je **juste veux un**
   I only want one

   J'en veux juste un
   I some want only one

   Intended Meaning: I only want one

6. Le chat **toujours mordre**
   The cat always to bite

   Le chat mord toujours
   bites always

   Intended Meaning: The cat always bites

7. **Avant** je vais . . .
   before I go (2nd sg.)

   Avant que j'aille . . .
   before that I go (subjunctive)

   Avant d'aller
   before of to go

   Intended Meaning: Before I go . . .

8. Un chalet où on va aller a
   a cottage where one goes to go to

   Un chalet où on va aller

   Intended Meaning: A cottage that we're going to go to

9. Le sac a un trou **dans le**
   the bag has a hole in it

   Il y a un trou dans le sac

   Intended Meaning 1. The bag has a hole in it; 2. There's a hole in the bag

10. Il veut moi de dire français à il
    He wants me to speak French to her

    Il veut que je lui parle français
    that to her speak

    Intended Meaning: He wants me to speak French to her

Questions

2. Describe instances of language transfer in these data. What evidence do you bring to bear in each case?

3. Is the same type of linguistic information being transferred in Part II as in Part I? Justify your answer with specific examples.

[1]Discernible from context.

Native Language: English
Target Language: French
Background Information: Immersion program, children ages 5 and 6
Data Source: Free conversation, picture description, and story-telling

Information about French: In French the normal word order for noun/adjective sequences is noun-adjective. However, some adjectives precede the noun. *Se sauver* is a reflexive verb and in the past tense is conjugated with the verb *être* (to be) rather than with the verb *avoir* (to have). *Avoir* is generally used in conjugating past tense with nonreflexive verbs. The subject pronoun is *il*. *Le* is an article and a direct object pronoun.

Data

Interlanguage	*Standard French*

1. une maison nouvelle   une nouvelle maison
   a   house   new

   Intended Meaning[1]: a new house

2. Je lis des histoires à il en français   Je lui lis des histoires en français
   I read some stories to him in French   I to him read some

   Intended Meaning: I read him stories in French

3. **Le** prend un . . . et après **le** prend l'autre   Il (en) prend un . . . et après il prend
   the take one   and after the takes the other   he some takes one   and after he takes

                                         l'autre
                                         the other

   Intended Meaning: He takes one and afterward he takes the other

4. Il a se sauvé   Il s' est sauvé
   He has refl. ran away ·   He refl. 3rd sg. to be ran away

   Intended Meaning: He ran away

Questions

1. Describe the IL data in each of the examples above.

2. What general explanation can be given to account for all the data?

*3. How can these results be reconciled with the results obtained in Problem 2.4, which come from the same data base?

---

[1]Discernible from context.

PROBLEM 2.6

Native Languages: English and French
Target Languages: French and English
Background Information: Adults
Data Source: Written compositions

======= Part I =======

Data

| *Interlanguage French L2* | *Standard French* |

1. **Tu assieds** sur une chaise
    you sit on a chair

    Tu t'assieds sur une chaise
    reflexive

    Intended Meaning[1]: You sit on a chair

2. Je vais **préparer** pour la fête
    I go to prepare for the party

    Je vais me préparer pour la fête
    reflexive

    Intended Meaning: I'm going to get ready for the party

3. Cette règle **applique** à tous
    this rule applies to all

    Cette règle s'applique a tous
    reflexive

    Intended Meaning: This rule applies to all

4. Elle **marche** les chats
    she walks the cats

    Elle promène les chats

    Intended Meaning: She walks the cats

| *Interlanguage English L2* | *Standard French* |

5. At sixty-five years old they must **retire themselves**

    . . . se retirer . . . (reflexive)

6. They want to **fight themselves** against this
    (tuition increase)

    . . . se battre . . . (reflexive)

Questions

1. Focus on the forms in boldface. Provide an IL description for these forms.

2. What do these examples suggest about lexical transfer? That is, what type(s) of lexical information is being transferred?

3. Does transfer seem to be bidirectional? That is, is the same type of lexical information being transferred from L1 to L2 in both language learning situations?

[1]Discernible from context.

Data

Interlanguage English L2   *Standard French*

1. They want to fight themselves **against** this (tuition   Ils   veulent se   battre contre cette (hausse)
   increase)   they want   refl. fight   against this

2. Physical fitness is **associated to** being good in   associé   a
   many   associated to

3. But feeling down or **suffering of** emotional pain   souffrer   de
                                                         to suffer of

Interlanguage French L2	*Standard French*	*Intended Meaning*[1]
4. **écouter à**	écouter NP	listen to
5. **regarder à**	regarder NP	look at
6. **entrer**	entrer dans (in)	enter
7. **chercher pour**	chercher NP	look for
8. **plaire**	plaire à (to)	please, like
9. **obéir**	obéir à (to)	obey
10. **payer pour**	payer NP	pay for
11. **échapper**	échapper à (to)	escape
12. **se souvenir**	se souvenir de	remember
	refl. remember of	

Questions

4. Focus on the forms in boldface. What do these examples suggest about lexical transfer? Compare your answer with that of Part I.

5. Does transfer seem to be bidirectional? Justify your answer.

*6. What additional evidence can you bring to bear, either from the literature on second language acquisition or from your own personal experience, which supports or refutes the concept of bidirectionality in L2 acquisition?

Part III

Data

Interlanguage French L2	Standard French

1. Je n'ai pas l'intention **de le** répondre   l'intention de lui répondre
   I neg have the intention of him answer   dat.

   Intended Meaning[1]: I don't intend to answer him

2. il **l'a**   besoin pour travailler   Il en a besoin pour travailler
   he it has need to   work   of it

   Intended Meaning: He needs it to work

3. Il a   dit a **Jean vendre** les livres   Il a dit a Jean de vendre les livres
   he pst. tell to Jean to sell the books   of

   Intended Meaning: He told Jean to sell the books

4. Nous ferons notre **mieux vous** donner   Nous ferons notre mieux de vous . . .
   we   will do our   best   you   give

   Intended Meaning: We will do our best to satisfy you

5. On n'a pas le **droit prendre** de l'un   et   On n'a pas le droit de prendre de l'un et de
   one neg has the right to take of the one and   of   of

   donner à l'autre   donner à l'autre
   to give to the other

   Intended Meaning: We haven't the right to take from one and give to the other

Interlanguage English L2	Intended Meaning

6. He stopped to defend himself   He stopped defending himself

7. We just enjoyed to move and to play   We just enjoyed moving and playing

Information about French: Gerundive complements do not exist in French.

Questions

7. What kind of L1 information is used in producing these L2 lexical forms?

8. Does the same type of information seem to be used by French L1 and English L1 speakers?

*9. What do the examples in this problem suggest about the organization of the mental lexicon and the type of lexical information which is transferred from the L1 to the L2?

---

[1]Discernible from context.

**10. How does lexical subcategorization affect L2 lexical acquisition?

Native Language: Dutch
Target Language: English
Background Information: 81 adults
Data Source: Judgments of translatability into English of the Dutch word *breken* "break." (Students were asked to judge whether the Dutch word *breken* could be translated by the English word *break*.)

Data

	Dutch sentence (all grammatical)	English equivalent	% of responses "translatable"
1.	Welk land heeft de wapenstilstand **gebroken**?	Which country has broken the ceasefire?	28
2.	Zij **brak** 't wereldrecord.	She broke the world record.	51
3.	Zij **brak** zijn hart	She broke his heart.	79
4.	De golven **braken** op de rotsen.	The waves broke on the rock.	35
5.	Hij **brak** zijn woord.	He broke his word.	60
6.	Hij **brak** zijn been.	He broke his leg.	81
7.	Het ondergrondse verzet werd **gebroken**.	The underground resistance was broken.	22
8.	Dankzij 'n paar grapjes was 't ijs eindelijk **gebroken**.	Thanks to a few jokes, the ice was finally broken.	33
9.	'n Spelletje zou de middag enigszins **breken**	A game would break up the afternoon a bit.	11
10.	Zijn val werd door 'n boom **gebroken**.	His fall was broken by a tree.	17
11.	't Kopje **brak**.	The cup broke.	64
12.	Nood **breekt** wet.	Necessity breaks law (a saying)	34
13.	Sommige arbeiders hebben de staking **gebroken**.	Some workers have broken the strike.	9
14.	Na 't ongeluk is hij 'n **gebroken** man geworden.	After the accident, he was a broken man.	61
15.	Zijn stem **brak** toen hij 13 was.	His voice broke when he was 13.	17
16.	De man **brak** zijn eed	The man broke his oath.	47
17.	De lichtstralen **breken** in het water.	The light rays refract in the water.	25

Questions

1. Order these sentences in terms of greater to lesser translatability of the Dutch word *breken*.

2. What differences are there in these sentences which might account for the varying degrees of translatability ascribed to them?

*3. What predictions can you make on the basis of these data concerning the acquisition of lexical meaning in an L2?

*4. How do you account for 81 percent acceptance for item 6, 79 percent for item 3, but only 64 percent for item 11?

PROBLEM 2.8

Native Languages: English, Spanish, Hungarian, Rumanian
Target Language: Hebrew
Background Information: University students, ages 17 to 26
Data Source: Fill in the blank test

Information about Hebrew: Hebrew has three words for "man" depending on the function of the word in context. The three words and their English equivalents are as follows:

    gever   (hero, macho)
    baal   (husband)
    iš   (man)

On the other hand, **iša** (woman, wife) serves all three functions.

    lsapeq means "provide"
    latet, general term meaning "give"
    limsor means "transmit"

Data

Hebrew sentences
1. hatnu'a hafeministit makira bahevdel šebein _____ la'iša.
2. bemešekh tequfat hašerut ḥayav cahal _____ laḥayal et kol corkav hafiziyim.
3. kešetagi'a habaita al tiškaḥ _____ drišat šalom lehorekha.

English translations
1. The feminist movement acknowledges the difference between _____ and women.
2. During his period of military service the Army must _____ the soldier with all his physical needs.
3. When you get home, don't forget to _____ regards to your parents.

Responses by NSs and NNSs

Sentence		NSs (n = 100)	NNSs (n = 100)
1	gever	98%	55%
	iš	1%	39%
2	lsapeq	89%	36%
	latet	9%	34%
3	limsor	100%	75%
	other	0%	25%

Questions

1. Describe the kinds of words that learners select as opposed to the words native speakers select.

2. The responses by NNSs to sentence 3 show a similar trend to NS responses. Does this sentence appear to be a counterexample to a more general trend?

3. If you were to learn that *limsor drišat šalom* is an expression meaning "give regards to," would that alter the conclusions you have come to thus far?

*4. What do these data suggest about the process of L2 lexical acquisition?

SECTION 3

Phonology

The concepts in this section are primarily linguistic ones and as such are not unique to issues in second language acquisition. A major concern in this regard is whether or not these same concepts are relevant to the analysis of IL data. A key concept that has not been introduced thus far is that of language universals. Within this section, language universals refers to aspects of language which are common to all languages.

Native Language: Arabic
Target Language: English
Background Information: Adults
Data Source: Mixed

======= Part I =======

Data

Below are examples of IL forms produced by speakers of two dialects of Arabic:

Egyptian speakers:
a.	[filoor]	"floor"
b.	[bilastik]	"plastic"
c.	[θirii]	"three"
d.	[tiransilet]	"translate"
e.	[silayd]	"slide"
f.	[firɛd]	"Fred"
g.	[čildiren]	"children"

Iraqi speakers:
a.	[ifloor]	"floor"
b.	[ibleen]	"plane"
c.	[isnoo]	"snow"
d.	[iθrii]	"three"
e.	[istadi]	"study"
f.	[ifrɛd]	"Fred"
g.	[čilidren]	"children"

Questions

1. Many Arabic speakers tend to insert a vowel in their pronunciation of English words. Based on these data, what vowel do they insert and where do they insert it?

2. State the rule or rules that describe the IL generalization these learners have come up with.

======= Part II =======

Data

These dialects also have rules inserting vowels in certain positions in native language words. The application of these rules is illustrated below.

1. Egyptian Arabic

katabu (katab+u)	"He wrote it/him"
katabtu (katab+t+u)	"I wrote it/him"
katablu (katab+l+u)	"He wrote to it/him"
katabtilu (katab+t+l+u)	"I wrote to it/him"

2. Iraqi Arabic

kitaba (kitab+a)	"He wrote it/him"
kitabta (kitab+t+a)	"I wrote it/him"
kitabla (kitab+l+a)	"He wrote to it/him"
kitabitla (kitab+t+l+a)	"I wrote to it/him"

Questions

3. State the rule(s) required to describe each Arabic dialect.

4. Compare these NL rules with the rules you arrived at to describe the speakers' IL forms in Part I. What conclusions can you draw from this comparison?

===== **Part III** =====

Data

Some exceptions to the rule(s) of Part I involve clusters of *s* plus certain consonants. Below are forms of Egyptian speakers:

a.	[istadi]	"study"
b.	[izbasyal]	"special"
c.	[iski]	"ski"

Questions

*5. Characterize the sequences of consonants which behave exceptionally.

*6. On the basis of what you know so far about Egyptian Arabic, can you explain the exceptional behavior found in question 5 as a result of transfer from the NL? If not, how might it be explained? You may find it useful to consider the following facts as well:

Turkish borrowings from English:	[tiren]	"train"
	[isport]	"sport"
Hindi borrowings from English:	[tiren]	"train"
	[iskul]	"school"

Native Language: Spanish
Target Language: English
Background Information: Adults
Data Source: Mixed

======= Part I =======

Data

Subject 1		Subject 2	
IL phonetic form	Gloss	IL phonetic form	Gloss
[bɔp]	Bob	[rav]	rob
[bɔbi]	Bobby	[ravər]	robber
[rɛt]	red	[bɔp]	Bob
[rɛðər]	redder	[bɔbi]	Bobby
[bik]	big	[smuθ]	smooth
[bigər ∿ biɣər]	bigger	[smuðər]	smoother
[bref]	brave	[rɛθ ∿ rɛð]	red
[brevər]	braver	[rɛðər]	redder
[prawt]	proud	[du]	do
[prawdəst]	proudest	[riðu]	redo
[wɛt]	wet	[bek]	bake
[wɛtər]	wetter	[priβek]	prebake
[sik]	sick	[wɛt]	wet
[sikəst]	sickest	[wɛtər]	wetter
[ðə]	the	[sef]	safe
[son]	zone	[sefəst]	safest
[fʌsi]	fuzzy	[ðə]	the
[faðər]	father	[ðis]	this
[fris]	freeze	[pig]	pig
[tæg]	tag	[bæd]	bad
[bɛd]	bed	[bɛt]	bed
[pɪg]	pig	[bik ∿ big ∿ biɣ]	big

Questions

1. Describe the phonetic alternations in these data.

2. What differences do you see between the two Spanish speakers in their IL phonetics?

*3. Where words have the same or a related gloss, provide an IL variable rule description.

================ **Part II** ================

Data

Subject 1		Subject 2	
IL underlying form	*Gloss*	*IL underlying form*	*Gloss*
/bɔb/	Bob	/rab/	rob
/bɔbi/	Bobby	/rabər/	robber
/rɛd/	red	/bɔb/	Bob
/rɛdər/	redder	/bɔbi/	Bobby
/big/	big	/smuð/	smooth
/bigər/	bigger	/smuðər/	smoother
/brev/	brave	/rɛd/	red
/brevər/	braver	/rɛdər/	redder
/prawd/	proud	/du/	do
/prawdəst/	proudest	/ridu/	redo
/wɛt/	wet	/bek/	bake
/wɛtər/	wetter	/pribek/	prebake
/sik/	sick	/wɛt/	wet
/sikəst/	sickest	/wɛtər/	wetter
/ðə/	the	/sef/	safe
/son/	zone	/sefəst/	safest
/fʌasi/	fuzzy	/ðə/	the
/faðər/	father	/ðis/	this
/fris/	freeze	/pig/	pig
/tæg/	tag	/bæd/	bad
/bɛd/	bed	/bɛd/	bed
/pɪg/	pig	/big/	big

Questions

*4. Comparing this table of underlying forms with the table in Part I, describe the assumptions that have to be made to create an IL list of underlying forms from a comparable list of IL phonetic data.

*5. What is the status of underlying forms in an IL and in ILs in general? What counterargument could one present to the creation of underlying forms of IL learning?

Native Language: Chinese (Mandarin)
Target Language: English
Background Information: Adults
Data Source: Mixed

Data

Subject 1		Subject 2	
IL phonetic form	Gloss	IL phonetic form	Gloss
[tæg ∿ tægə]	tag	[ænd ∿ ændə]	and
[rab ∿ rabə]	rob	[hæd ∿ hædə]	had
[hæd ∿ hæsə]	had	[tɔb ∿ tɔbə]	tub
[hiz ∿ hizə]	he's	[staɽ ɪd ∿ staɽ ɪdə]	started
[smuðə]	smoother	[fiʊd ∿ fiʊdə]	filled
[rayt]	right	[bɪg ∿ bɪgə]	big
[dɛk]	deck	[rɛkənayzdə]	recognized
[zɪp]	zip	[ɪz ∿ ɪzə]	is
[mɪs]	miss	[sɛz ∿ sɛzə]	says
[wɛt]	wet	[wɔtə]	water
[dɪfər]	differ	[afə]	offer
[ovər]	over	[lidə]	leader
[bɪgər]	bigger		
[kɪkɪn]	kicking		
[tægɪn]	tapping		
[lebər]	label		
[lɛtər]	letter		
[blidɪn]	bleeding		
[lidə]	leader		

Questions

1. Describe the phonetic alternations in these data.

2. What differences do you see between the two Chinese speakers in their IL phonetics?

*3. Where words have the same or a related gloss, provide an IL variable rule description.

*4. What underlying forms would you propose for these data? Follow the format set up below:

Subject 1		Subject 2	
IL underlying form	Gloss	IL underlying form	Gloss
/tæg/	tag	/ænd/	and

*5. What assumptions did you have to make to create an IL list of underlying forms from the IL phonetic data?

*6. What is the status of underlying forms in an IL and in ILs in general? What counterargument could one present to the creation of underlying forms in IL learning?

**7. Compare your results in this problem on the phonetics of Chinese-English with those obtained looking at parallel data in Problem 3.2 on the phonetics of Spanish-English. How does this comparison affect your answer in question 6?

PROBLEM 3.4

Native Language: Japanese
Target Language: English
Background Information: Adults
Data Source: Free speech, dialogue reading, word list reading

══════ Part I ══════

Data

Variants of /r/ by Japanese learners of English
[ɽ̆]   voiced nonretroflexed flap
[l̆]   voiced lateral flap
[l]   voiced lateral
[ř]   voiced retroflexed flap
[r]   voiced retroflexed semiconsonant

Information about Japanese: Japanese has an /r/ phoneme, but not a phoneme /l/. /r/ is phonetically realized as [ř]. [l̆] is an allophonic variant of /r/.

Questions

1. Japanese learners typically use the above variants for English /r/. How would you describe the phonetic substitutions they make?

══════ Part II ══════

Data

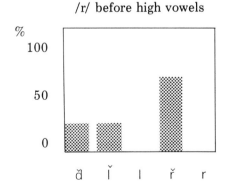
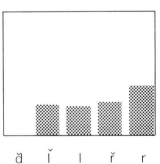
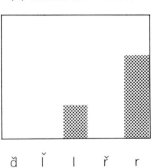

Questions

2. What do the above bar graphs suggest about the role of the phonetic environment in phonetic learning?

53

3. In addition to different phonetic variants, what else does vowel height affect?

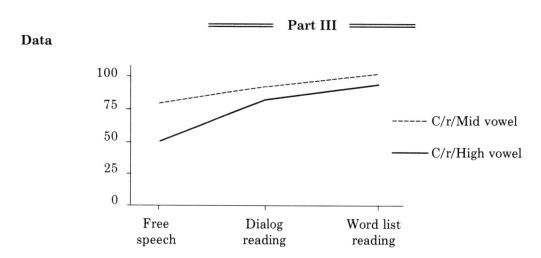

Data

Part III

100
75
50
25
0

------ C/r/Mid vowel

———— C/r/High vowel

Free speech   Dialog reading   Word list reading

Questions

4. Consider the above graph, which represents phonetic [ɾ] in two environments. What does it suggest about the interaction of the phonetic environment and a specific speech style?

5. Given the data presented thus far, what conclusions can you draw about the systematic nature of phonetic variants of English /r/ by Japanese speakers?

PROBLEM 3.5

Native Languages: Korean, Chinese (Cantonese) and Portuguese
Target Language: English
Background Information: Adults
Data Source: Picture descriptions

Part I

Data

Korean I. IPA Transcription

ɑiθɪŋ:kə̆ʃi:mes:æmɪtʃə̆ ... t̠ɛn:pʊtŋəsæke ... ðɛn:ə̆ ... ʃigo ... ʔɑuʔ ...
t̠ẽʃiwɔʔ ... t̠ẽʃidrɔp̚' ... ʃidrɔp̚' ... əʃisɪ:sʌmples: ... ə̆ŋə̆kə̆lɑsɔi:sʌmples ...
ɑiɪlidonowʌrɪʃiduɪŋ ... t̠ɛn ... ʔə ... ʃi ... pʊtŋəʔɪnsɛk̚ 't̠ə̆tʃɛk̚ 't̠əsɛʔ ...
ʔə̆zə̆ho: ... t̠ə̆sɑ:ə̆sæmɪtʃə̆gɔ̃ ... ɔlgɔ̃ ... zədɔə̆ʔit̚' ... lʊkslɑikə̆dɔə̆'fʌn ...

Gloss of Transcription

I thinka she ma(kes) sammitcha... then put'n a sackay... then uh... she go... ou(t)... the(n) she
wa(lk)... the(n) she drop... she drop? uh she si(ts) someplace... in a c/ə/lass or someplace... I
really don'know what is she doing... then... uh... she... out'n a in sack to check the sa(ck)... is a
ho(le)... the sa... uh sammitcha go(ne)... all go(ne)... the dog eat... looks like a dog fun...

Korean II. IPA Transcription

ʃime:əsæmɪtʃi ... ʃimekɪŋ ... əsæmɪʔ ... æn:ʃipʊrɪn: ... pepɚbæi ...
æn:ʃitek̚'ɑu: ... ŋʃiyoʔwɔkɪŋno ... ɑiθɪnt̠ẽ ... ʃigosʌmə̆sku:ɚsʌmðɪŋ ...
æn:ʃi ... ʔn:ʃidrɔp̚' ... sæms: ... so ... ʃi ... ʃipʊrɪnəbæ: ... t̠ə:pepɚhæs:
... ʔə ... ho: ... so ... ʃi ... sɚpɪʔm ... s ... ʔm̩ ... o: ... ʃisi: ...
ʔə̃hosæ̃:ʔɪʃsæ̃wɪtʃi: ... dɔʔ ... dɔ:ə̆'it ... hɚsæ̃wɪtʃə̆ ...

Gloss of Transcription

She ma(kes) a sammitchy... she making... a sammi(tch)... an' she put in... paper ba(g)... an'
she take ou(t)... 'n she go walking, no? I thin(k) the(n)... she go somea schoo(l) or something... an'
she... 'n she drop... sams... so... she... she put in a ba(g)... the paper has... a... ho(le)... so
... she... surpr... um... s... m... oh... she see... a ho(le) sa, i, sa(nd)witchy... do(g)... dog
eat... her sa(nd)witcha...

Cantonese I. IPA Transcription

t̠ə̆gɚɣznemɪs ... dʒɔ̃: ... ʔæn: ... ʃiʒgoɪŋ ... ʔə:tuhævə̆pɪʔŋik̚' ... æn: ...
fɚsʔəvʔɔ: ... ʃiə̆pʔ ... pɪpɛɚs:əʔdʒæm:sæ̃wɪtʃə̆ ... æn: ... ʃipʊʔsɪʔɪnə̆bæ:k ...
ʔə̆m ... ʃibɪɪŋ:z ... ʔəm ... sæ̃miʃ ... ʔænəʔ ... blæŋkə̆tə̆ ... wɪθhɚanə̆wei:
... æn: ... sʌdŋli ... ʃi ... dɪɔps ... t̠əsæ̃wɪtʃə̆ ... bəʃidʌzə̆noðæʔ ... æn: ...
wẽʃi ... ɪɪtʃəz:ðə̆ples?ə̃ ... wɛɚʃi ... pɪænstuhævə̆ pɪʔŋikə̆ ... ʃiə̆spɪɛʔ ...
spɪɛʔs:t̠ə̆biæŋkə̆ts ... ʔɑn ... ʔanə̆gɪɑu: ... ænt̠ɛ ... ʃiteksɑurə̆sæ̃wɪtʃə̆ ... bʌʔ
... ʃidɪskʌvɚt̠æt̠'əsæ̃wɪtʃə̆wəzgɔ̃:ŋ ... æn ... ʃidə̆zŋoʔwɑi: ... æn ... ðærə̆zb̥kʌz
... ʔəm: ... ʃidɪɔpsɪt̠ʔɑnə̆wei:ən ... t̠ə̆dɔʔ ... dɔgʔz ... gɛʔ ... gerə̆tə̆ ...

Gloss of Transcription

The girl's name is... Joa(n)... an'... she's going... uh to have a pi(c)nic... an' firs(t) of a(ll)... she
uhp... p(r)epares a jam sa(nd)witcha... an'... she puts i(t) in a bag... um... she brings... um...
samish... an' a... blanketa... with her n (th)e way... an'... suddenly... she... drops... the
sa(nd)witcha... bu(t) she doesn't know tha(t) an'... whe(n) she... reaches the place uh... where
she... prans to have a pi(c)nica... she uh sprea... sorea /ʔ/ s the brankets... on... on (th)e
grou(nd)... an' the(n)... she takes out a sa(nd)witcha... bu(t)... she discover(s) that (th)e
sa(nd)witcha was gone... an'... she doesn' know why... an'... that is b'cause... 'um... she drops
it on (th)e way an'... the do(g)... dogs... ge... get ita...

Cantonese II. IPA Transcription

ʔəgɚːɪsɑː ... fɪsɪŋhɚtoːs ... wɪf ... dʒæm ... ænɑifɪŋɑːʃiistrɑintuːhæfəpɪʔnɪʔt' ... ænhig' ... ænhihæʔ ... ʔænhihæʔ ... ænə̃ʃihæsʔɛvifɪŋ ... ɪɛdiænə ... ʃiwə ... ʃiwəsohæpiə̯n ... gɛtɪŋʔɑuəvt̯ə̃dɔə ... æn ... ʃiwɑsoː ... sʔʃʔ ... (unintelligible) ʃiwɔkə̃lɔŋt̯əioːæn ... ə̃nʃididə̃no ... ɛə ... t̯ə ... t̯əsæʔwəs' ... wəs' ... ʔə̃ ... ə̃ʃ ... ʃidɪːŋːotɪsəʔ ... notɪst̯æt̯ə̃sæt'ə ... wɛs'bɪokænə̃t̯ə sæ̃wɪtʃə̃kemɑut ... ænə ... hi ... higotut̯t̯əbitʃænə̃peːwɪfəsæn ... æn ... ɑftəːwɑiɣʃiːfɛlt'hæʔhʌŋgiiʔænʃiwɑnts ... ʃiwʌntətuʔɪtʔsʌmsæ̃wɪtʃə̃ ... ænə ... ʃitʊkɑutəsætə̃ʔə̃n ... ʃifɑuŋɑut̯ətisɛt̯ə̃ ... wəsbɪokə̃ ... ænə ... æ ənʃiwəsːə̃n ... ʃiwəsə̃nɑʔʃuɚwɛɚ ... wɛɚʃilɔst̯ə̃sæ̃wɪtʃə̃z ... æn ... ænɑntʃiʔʌt̯əhænə ... t̯idɔ-sɑɚʔitɪŋ ... hɚsæ̃wɪtʃə̃z ...

Gloss of Transcription

A gir(l) is uh... fixing her toas(t)... wif... jam... an' I thin(k) uh she is tryin' to have a pi(c)nic... an' he g... an' he ha... an' he ha'... an' uh she has everything... ready an' uh... she wa... she was so happy an'... getting ou(t) of the doo(r)... an'... she was so... s, sh... (unintelligible) she walk along the roa(d) an'... 'mshe didn' know uh... the... the sa(ck) was... was... uh... uh, sh... she di(dn't) noticea... notice that (th)e sack uh... was broken a(nd) the sa(nd)witcha came out... an' uh... he... he go to the beach an' uh p(l)ay wif (tha)sa(nd)... an'... afte(r) while she felt ha, hungry an' she wants... she wanted to eat some sa(nd)witcha... an' uh... she took out (th)a sacka an' she found ou(t) tha(t) the sacka... was brokea... an' uh... a, an' she wasn'... she wasa no(t) sure where ... where she los(t) (th)e sa(nd)witches... an'... an' on the other han(d)a... the do(g)s are eating ... her sa(nd)witches

Portuguese I. IPA Transcription

ðigɚə̃l ... pɪkʌp ... æːbɔn ... æn ... piipɛɚdəhiz ... ə ... fudfɔɚ ... hɚfudfɔɚ ... əːpikənik ... əː ... hwɛn ... ʔhi ... wʌzgoiŋtuðəpɪkənik ... ʃiː ... lɑstə̃ ... hɚs ... sɑndəwiʃ ... æn ... ʃi ... ʃidʌsəntə̃n ... noəbɑut'it ... æn ... hwɛ̃ːs ... ʃi ... ərɑivtə̃ðəplesə̃ʔwɛɚ ... ʃiwɑntugo ... ʔə ... ʃi ... pʊtə ... ʔə ... bæŋkə̃tə̃ ... ðəflɔɚ ... ænpiipɛɚtuit' ... bʌt' ... hwɛ̃hi ... gɛtəhɚːbæg ... ʃi ... ʔɛː ... notə̃ðæt ... hɚbægə̃wʌs ... bə̃ɪokən ... ænðætʃilɔstə̃ ... hɚ ... sænwɪʃ' ... ænʃiː ... bikemzvɛɚs ... oː ... sɚpiɑizdə̃ ... ænə ... ðəfɚsθɪŋ ... ðəkemztuhɚmɑinːəzðæt ... sʌɪndɔgz ... wʌːzitɪŋ ... hɚfud ...

Gloss of Transcription

The girl... pick up... aah, bun... an' prepareda his... uh... food for... her food for... a picanic ... uh... when... he... was going to the picanic... she... losta... her s... sandawish... an'... she... she doesn'ta n... know about it... an'... whe(n) s... she... arrive to the placea where... she want to go... uh... she... puta uh... b(l)anketa... the floor... an' prepare to eat... but... whe(n) he geta her bag... she... eh... notea that... her baga was... baroken... an' that she losta ... her... sanwish... an' she... becames ver's... oh... surpriseda... an' uh... the firs' thing... tha(t) cames to her min(d) is that some dogs... was eating... food

Portuguese II. IPA Transcription

suziʔwʌzə̃gudə ... vɛiivɛiigudəgɚl ... ʃi ... ʃilɑik' ... ʃilɑikʔit' ... vɛiimʌtʃ'bikʌzʃizfæt ... ʃizʌɛritæt ... ændə ... wʌndeiʃi ... wʌndeʃipiipɛɚmɛnisænwɪʃ ... fɔigotə̃ðskul ... sndiː ... hwɛnt̯ə̃bigin ... ʔəː ... hwɛ̃hwɛ̃ hwɛ̃nə̃bigin ... tuwɔk' ... ɪnziː ... hwɛnə̃bigintuwɔkə̃ ... ɪnðəfɔist' ... ʔəʔɪʔint̯igɑidən ... inti ... intʔ'ʔintigɑidən ... ʃiʃilɑstə̃də̃tii ... tsænwɪʃ ... oi ... ʃigotə̃dihɑuzə ... ænəbiginvɛiivɛiihʌŋii ... vɛiivɛi hʌŋii ... ænə̃ʃiciɑivɛiimʌtʃ' ... bʌt' ... vɳ ... ʃə̃ ... ə̃bʌʔə ... ʃiciɑivɛiivɛiimʌtʃ' ... bʌtəti ... tə̃ ... ʃihɑɛvə̃ ... tiː ... dɔgzːzistiitə̃dɔgz ... hævə̃tiyɑidən ... itə̃tilʌntʃ ... ænipænsvɛiivɛiiwɛl ...

Gloss of Transcription

Susie was a gooda... very very gooda girl... she... she like... she like eat... very much because she's fat... she's very fat... and uh... one day she... one day she prepare many sanwish... for go to the school . . . and, ee . . . when the begin . . . uh . . . whe, whe . . . when (sh)e begin . . . to walk . . . in the . . . when (sh)e begin to walka . . . in the forest . . . uh, i, in the garden . . . in the . . . int, in the garden . . . she, she losta the t(h)ree . . . sanwish . . . oh . . . she go to the housea . . . an' a begin very very hungry . . . very very hungry . . . an' ah she cry very much . . . but . . . m . . . ya . . . uh but uh . . . she cry very very much but uh ti . . . the . . . she havea . . . the . . . dogs the streeta dogs . . . have i(n) the garden . . . eata the lunch . . . an' (h)e pan(t)s very very well . . .

Questions

1. Categorize the syllable structure errors (from the point of view of the TL) in terms of (1) epenthesis and (2) consonant deletion for both final consonants and consonant clusters.

2. What is the percentage of syllable structure errors of these two error types as a function of total syllables attempted?

3. Do speakers of different languages make different types of syllable structure errors? Is the type of error dependent on whether or not it is a final consonant or consonant cluster?

4. What is the general strategy that is being used to deal with syllables in English?

====== **Part II** ======

Data

Information about the syllable structure of the native languages of the subjects:

Korean:
Open syllables

Cantonese:
Open syllables; most syllables are CV; some closed syllables, although only a limited number of consonants can be in syllable final position; consonant clusters across syllable boundaries

Portuguese:
Open syllables; most syllables are CV; limited number of consonants possible in syllable final position; some consonant clusters within a syllable

Some possible NL sequences:

Korean:	*Cantonese:*	*Portuguese:*
kɪts'ɑ	dzon	problemɑ
ko:l	mɑtɛɔɪ	iguɑl
sɑldzidɑ	kɑt	sueño
kɑn	sɛ:tsi	eʃtrɑɲo
sæk	ŋoʰwɑ:	
kəktɑ	ut	
tsuye ɪt	sæk tsæt	
ut	tɛɑu i:u	
kuəl	teŋiɑt iɑnwɑi	
ko:l	lɑi ɑ:	
oɑtɑ w	kɑ iɑtko	

Questions

*5. What percentage of the errors from Part I can be attributed to the NL?

*6. For those that are not attributable to the NL, how can they be explained?

*7. How much consistency is there between the two speakers of each language?

Native Language: Buryat (Soviet Union)
Target Language: Russian
Background Information: Adolescents and adults
Data Source: Spontaneous utterances

Information about Buryat: Buryat has a restricted syllable structure. There are no consonant clusters at the beginning or end of any syllable. Clusters can only arise in the middle of a word, with the first consonant grouped with the preceding vowel in one syllable and the second consonant grouped with the following vowel in another syllable. Furthermore, no Buryat word can begin with /r/.

Data

IL pronunciation	Russian pronunciation	Gloss
xabartir	kvartira	apartment
šorta	čort	devil
aperxa	afrika	Africa
piriznal	priznal	recognized
streča	vstreča	meeting
arbočij	rabočij	worker
moldoj	molodoj	young
birgardir	brigadir	brigadier
boles'	bolezn'	illness
taraja	vtoraja	second
staval	vstaval	got up
kürgøm	krugom	round

Questions

1. What phonological processes (e.g., deletion) are involved in the relationship between the IL forms and the target language forms?

2. Is there a way of predicting which processes will take place in any given instance? (a) If so, what predictions can be made? (b) If not, can any predictions be made about the relationship between TL and IL forms?

Native Language: Thai
Target Language: English
Background Information: Nine adult subjects
Data Source: Free conversation and reading of word lists

Part I

Data

IL variant		Speech style			
		Conversation		Listing	
		No.	%	No.	%
Initial R					
ɹ	TL variant (correct)	30	38.5	4	8.9
ɹˈ		40	51.3	5	11.1
ɹ̥		2	2.6		
ɹ̃	new	3	3.8	15	33.3
wɹˈ	variants			1	2.2
⊤				2	4.4
ɭ				1	2.2
ǀ				3	6.7
ř	NL variants (interference)	3	3.8	3	6.7
r̃				11	24.4
	Totals:	78	100%	45	99.9%
Final R					
ɹ	TL variants	9	4.6		
ɹˈ	(correct)	72	36.5	13	72.2
∅	possible NL	65	33	3	16.7
ə	interference	49	24.9	2	11.1
w	new variant	2	1.1		
	Totals:	197	100.1%	18	100%

Key to the IL Phonetic Variants of R

ɹ   a retroflex continuant; considered correct (native) in initial or final position in American English; not native to Thai (but occasionally borrowed as an initial)

ɹˈ   a more open, less retroflex, continant; considered correct (native New York English) in final position, but incorrect in initial position; not native to Thai

ɹ̥   a voiceless retroflex continuant; initial position IL variant

ɹ̃   a retroflex, post-alveolar fricative; initial position IL variant

wɹˈ   an /ɹ/ preceded by the English labio-velar continuant /w/; initial position IL variant

ř   a rolled fricative; initial position IL variant

61

| | a retroflex, post-alveolar lateral; initial position IL variant
| ! | an apico-alveolar or denti-alveolar clear lateral with a flap-like quality due to tense articulation and more sudden release than American /l/; initial IL variant transferred from Thai
| ř | an apico-alveolar flap; initial position IL variant transferred from Thai
| ř | an apico-alveolar trill; initial position IL variant transferred from Thai
| ∅ | a zero sound for post-vocalic R; final position IL variant either transferred from Thai or acquired from an "r-less" dialect of English; usually accompanied by vowel lengthening on the immediately preceding vowel
| ə | a mid-central vowel; final position IL variant either transferred from the Thai rendition of loanwords or acquired from an "r-less" dialect of English
| w | a labio-velar continuant; final position IL variant

Questions

1. Given the distribution of the pronunciation of R in the above data, what is the major factor which determines which variant is selected by these Thai speakers?

2. Is it the same for both initial and final R's?

3. If your answer to 2 is no, what might be the cause of the difference? (Consider that these Thai speakers lived in New York, where it is common to drop postvocalic R, producing either /∅/ or /ə/. Consider also that Thai does not have final R.)

=== Part II ===

Data

| | Speech style | |
Cause of error	Conversation	Listing
Initial R [ř], [ř̃], [!]	6.2%	39.4%
New variants [ɹ'], [wɹ'], [ɹ̟], [ɹ̠], [r], [l̩]	93.8%	60.6%
Final R[1]		

[1]Final R does not exist in the NL (Thai). Therefore, the distinction between NL interference and TL approximation (new variants) cannot be maintained.

Questions

4. What do these data suggest about the use of NL variants?

5. What explanation can you give for there being more NL variants in a reading of word lists than in free conversation?

=== **Part III** ===

Data

IL use of two variants of R

	ř	r̃
Conversation	3.8%	0%
Listing	6.7%	24.4%

Native Language Information: In careful speech Thais use /ř/ (which they consider to be "correct" R). However, in the most formal settings, they use /r̃/.

Questions

6. How can you account for the use of different varieties of R in different contexts?

*7. What do these data suggest about the use of other than phonetic factors in the interpretation of L2 data?

SECTION 4

Syntax/Semantics

In this section, we refer to concepts which have already been dealt with in earlier sections, e.g., developmental progression, language transfer, language universals. We also introduce some new concepts:

1. Prefabricated patterns
2. Formulas
3. Formulaic sentence frames
4. Core meanings
5. Fossilization

Prefabricated patterns are essentially the same as unanalyzed units discussed in Section 1.

Formulas refer to language which functions wholly (or partially) as unanalyzed units (cf. Section 1).

Formulaic sentence frames refer to templates which may be used in sentence production. Different information is fitted into a fixed slot. For example, "How about a movie?" "How about a cookie?" consist of a formula "how about" plus an NP.

Core meanings are those meanings of a word/grammatical form which are the most common or the most basic. In essence, they constitute the prototypical meaning.

Fossilization refers to a cessation of IL learning, often far from TL norms.

PROBLEM 4.1

Native Language: Arabic
Target Language: English
Background Information: Three subjects, intermediate to advanced
Data Source: Compositions and conversations

Part I

Data

1. **She give** me almost everyday a lesson.
2. **He understand.**
3. The **air-conditioning refuse** to work.
4. And **the other** just **come** to buy and leave.
5. So **nobody have** time to be your friend.
6. When **he complete** nine month.
7. **There is many things.**
8. **There is many kind** of way you can make baklawa.
9. **Many vocabulary** I don't know what **it means.**

Questions

1. Describe the agreement that occurs between nouns and verbs in the above data.

2. How does this differ from standard English usage?

Part II

Data

1. **They are** very surprised.
2. **Many people** here **have** a braces.
3. First of all, when **you are** approaching King Abdul Aziz Airport.
4. **Every Moslem knows** that Jeddah is the starting place for making the pilgrimage to Mecca.
5. **It's size is** about one million by 1200 square kilometers from north to south.
6. **He speaks** Arabic without accent.
7. And **the other man who likes** to stand on trash cans.
8. You make sure this from the way **he talks.**
9. They say **this is** wrong.
10. **They are** swing.

Questions

3. The above sentences produced by the same students appear to be correct in terms of target language N-V agreement. How does this affect your IL generalization(s) in Part I?

*4. What additional data would you like to elicit from these students?

PROBLEM 4.2

Native Language: Japanese
Target Language: English
Background Information: English Language Institute students in Hawaii
Data Source: Student compositions and informant feedback

Part I

Data

1. There are some people **to get married several times**.
2. When I went down the street, I found a poster **to advertise the coming dance concert**.
3. There are some differences **to represent the national character**.
4. I've planned to have a farewell party for a friend **to go to the mainland**.
5. There are many boys **to like baseball in Japan**.
6. In a cafeteria we will take the dish **to want to eat**.
7. We can go to places **to want to go faster by using a car**.

Questions

1. In the first five examples, the assumed subject of the infinitive modifiers appears immediately to the left of the infinitive, i.e., in 1 "people" get married, etc. What are the assumed subjects in 6 and 7?

2. Come up with an IL generalization(s) for the placement of infinitive modifiers for these data.

3. Provide TL semantic interpretations for these sentences and relate these to your answer to question 1.

Part II

Data

NNSs intended meaning (determined in playback interviews) for sentence:
2. "While I was walking down the street, I ran across a poster advertising the upcoming dance concert."
3. "There are some differences which represent the national character."
5. "There are many boys who like baseball in Japan."

*4. How does your interpretation of sentences 2, 3, and 5 (from question 3) differ from the meaning intended by the NNS?

**5. What other information would you like to elicit from these learners to test your hypotheses? Relate your answers when possible to data in Problem 1.1, where other infinitive modifiers also occur.

PROBLEM 4.3

Native Language: Japanese
Target Language: English
Background Information: Adult, high intermediate
Data Source: Compositions

Part I

Data

Once upon a time there was a man who called "Taro Urashia" in small village in Japan. One day, when he take a walk near his home, he help one turtle on the seaside. Since he helped the turtle, he was able to get a chance to be invited from sea castle which is deep place in the sea.

He had been entertained with music, good board, dance etc. every nights by beautiful girls of sea castle.

Therefore, he forgot worldly presence and he did not notice how long did he stay there.

Nevertheless he missed the new world, so he said that he wanted to go back to true world.

Questions

1. Concentrate on the use of articles in this composition. Is there a pattern to the use or lack of use of English articles by this learner? If so, what is it?

2. Is there a difference between the use of definite and indefinite articles? If so, what generalizations is this learner making about the use of definite vs. indefinite articles in English?

Part II

Data

I will tell you why I want to live in country better than in city. I live in suburb where is near Tokyo, and many people just return to my city for sleep. I know both city and country. Both they have good points and bad points, but I prefer to live in country.

I like nature, so I choose country. There are many inconvenient things, if I live in country. However I prefer nature better than convenience. I don't like narrow space, because I think it's not good for children, also our mind. Furthermore, I like quiet place.

If I live in country, I don't have opportunity to enjoy entertainment. Also, education system is not so good as city. That's a problem. It is difficult to say exactly I want to live in country. If there is a possibility to live in suburb. I prefer it, because we can have both side.

I can say I don't want to live in city. My idea for city is enjoyable place, but not to live. If I live in city, I will have frustration. Also I guess, relationship in city is those difficult than in country.

If I have only two choice, I prefer country. I've never thought to live in city. Actually, city is fun, but I don't want to live in city. I want to keep my mind peacefully.

Questions

3. The composition in Part II was written by a high intermediate Japanese speaker (different from the speaker in Part I). Is there a pattern to the use or lack of use of English articles by this learner? If so, what is it?

4. Is there a difference between the use of definite and indefinite articles? If so, what generalizations is this learner making about the use of definite vs. indefinite articles in English?

*5. Compare the use of articles by the speaker in Part I with the use of articles by the speaker in Part II. Is there a single generalization that you can come up with to describe article usage by these two Japanese speakers, or does each individual create her own IL generalization?

**6. Gather compositions from speakers of various NLs at different levels of proficiency. Do individual analyses, NL group analyses, proficiency level analyses of article usage. What similarities/differences do you find among individuals, NLs, and proficiency?

PROBLEM 4.4

Native Language: Japanese
Target Language: English
Background Information: Child, age 5:4 to 6:5
Data Source: Spontaneous speech

Part I

Data

Month 1
Do you know?
How do you do it?
Do you have coffee?
Do you want this one?

Month 2
What do you doing, this boy?
What do you do it, this, froggie?
What do you doing?
What do you drinking, her?

Questions

1. What is the relationship between the way questions are formed in Month 1 and in Month 2?

2. What kind of generalization has this child made about forming questions in English during Month 2?

3. What does her knowledge at Month 2 imply about her knowledge at Month 1?

Part II

Data

Contexts Requiring Past Auxiliary *did* in Question Form

Month	Unmarked	Marked
3	Why do you do? How do you make? How do you draw that?	
4	What do you do?	Where did you get that?

(continued on p. 74)

Month	Unmarked	Marked
5	How do you break it?	What did she say? What did you say? What did you say?
6	Do you bought too? Do you bought this too? Do you put it? Do you put it? How do you put it? How do you put it?	What did you do? What did you say?
7	How do you do it?	How did you get it?
8	Do you saw these peppermint? Do you saw some star eye? Do you saw some star eye?	Did you call? Did everybody saw some blue hairs?
9		Did you see the ghost? Did you know we locked the door when we come to here?
10		Did you use some blue? Why did you do that? Why did you get this? Why did you go to a hospital? Why did you draw?
11		What did you say? What did camel say? Did I made that? Did I make that? Did you see that? Did you see me? Why did you put this? I didn't correct this one, did I?
12		Did you what?

Questions

4. What can you determine from the data in Part II about this child's acquisition of past tense question formation?

*5. Is the acquisition of the past auxiliary in questions a case of all or nothing, or does acquisition appear to be gradual? What evidence can you bring to bear to support your conclusions (cf. Problem 4.7, question 7)?

PROBLEM 4.5

Native Language: Arabic
Target Language: English
Background Information: Three subjects, intermediate to advanced
Data Source: Compositions and conversation

Part I

Data

1. You know what's baklawa?
2. You know what's the problem?
3. You know Washington Street?
4. You know Mufida?
5. He said this about me?

Questions

1. Describe the way in which these learners form questions in English.

2. How do these data compare with TL question formation?

Part II

Data

1. What you said you like to make?
2. What did you learn doing?
3. What you call?
4. What you mean, kids?
5. What can make?
6. Where your house?
7. Where she is from?
8. Why this "Khalwa" funny name?
9. How many you have?
10. How you can hang it?

Questions

3. What IL patterns have these students developed for asking wh- questions?

*4. Compare the pattern of question formation in Part I with these patterns.

===== **Part III** =====

Data

1. Did you do the laundry?
2. Did you sleep yesterday night?
3. Did you drive your car?
4. Did your parents take care of you?
5. Did you shop today?
6. Do you like your apartment?
7. Do you love your children?
8. Do you have money?
9. Do you come every day to Tower Plaza?
10. Do you were her teacher?

Questions

**5. Keep in mind that the data from Parts I, II, and II were elicited from the same three subjects. Compare the way questions are formed in the three sets of data.

**6. If any of these data appear to be more like TL patterns, what IL generalization could account for this?

**7. Compare your results from this problem with those from Problem 4.4. What similarities/differences do you find between the Japanese child's acquisition of question formation and these Arabic adults' acquisition of question formation?

PROBLEM 4.6

Native Language: Spanish
Target Language: English
Background Information: Child
Data Source: Spontaneous utterances

Part I

Data

1. Lookit, like that.
2. Looky, chicken.
3. Hey look dese.
4. Lookit four cars.
5. Look two cars.
6. Lookit gas.
7. Lookit there.
8. Lookit four.
9. Hey look, lunch money.

Questions

1. In the above data, what evidence is there for the existence of formulaic sentence frames?

2. What sentence frame(s) do you propose for these data?

3. What function does the sentence frame appear to have?

Data

1. Is putting it dese.
2. Is making it the car.
3. Is putting the shoes.
4. Make it dese.
5. Is got it dese one.
6. Is got it un truck.

Questions

4. At the time of these utterances, the child began to produce VPs which functioned as sentence frames, e.g., Is it . . . ? What is the function of *it* in the sentences above? Justify your answer.

*5. Turn to Appendix I and describe the additional data set for this problem. Reevaluate your answers to questions 1 to 4 above in light of these additional data. What do the data in this problem and in the appendix suggest about the acquisition of L2 syntax and about the possible role of fossilization in L2 acquisition?

PROBLEM 4.7

Native Languages: Spanish, Japanese
Target Language: English
Background Information: Adult learners (52 Spanish and 37 Japanese)
Data Source: Grammaticality judgments

Information from a Cross-Linguistic Perspective: (1) Core (basic) meaning for progressives is: ongoing, witnessed activity which persists for an extended period of time. (2) Core (basic) meaning for simple present is: lawlike regular state or expectable events characteristic of their subject at the present time. (3) Core (basic) meaning for future is: states or events expected in foreseeable future.

Part I

Data

		Spanish speakers (n = 52) *% "correct" judgments*
1.	Dan sees better.	65
2.	Dan is seeing better now.	81
3.	Mary is being in Chicago now.	8
4.	John is travelling to New York tomorrow.	8
5.	The new bridge connects Detroit and Windsor.	79
6.	The new bridge is connecting Detroit and Windsor.	46
7.	John travels to New York tomorrow.	8
8.	John will travel to New York tomorrow.	86
9.	John is smoking American cigarettes now.	88
10.	The new bridge will connect Detroit and Windsor.	67
11.	Fred smokes American cigarettes now.	56
12.	Mary will be in Chicago now.	10
13.	John will smoke American cigarettes now.	10
14.	Mary is in Chicago now.	88

Questions

1. Focus on the three verb tense/aspect elements: (1) progressive, (2) simple present, (3) future. For each, order the sentences from those judged "most correct" to those judged "least correct." What explanation can you give for the differential acceptability of the various uses of each tense/aspect?

*2. What do these data suggest about the interaction between syntax and semantics in second language acquisition?

*3. Consider sentences 4 and 7, the translation equivalents of which are possible in Spanish. The acceptability of these sentences in English is low. How can you account for this?

**4. What does this suggest about the interaction between language transfer and language universal facts? You may want to relate your discussion on this question to your discussion of Problem 2.7.

═══ **Part II** ═══

Data

		Japanese speakers (n = 37) % "correct" judgments
1.	Dan sees better.	43
2.	Dan is seeing better now.	19
3.	Mary is being in Chicago now.	5
4.	John is travelling to New York tomorrow.	32
5.	The new bridge connects Detroit and Windsor.	73
6.	The new bridge is connecting Detroit and Windsor.	24
7.	John travels to New York tomorrow.	19
8.	John will travel to New York tomorrow.	81
9.	John is smoking American cigarettes now.	76
10.	The new bridge will connect Detroit and Windsor.	87
11.	Fred smokes American cigarettes now.	51
12.	Mary will be in Chicago now.	14
13.	John will smoke American cigarettes now.	3
14.	Mary is in Chicago now.	92

Questions

5. Focus on the three verb tense/aspect elements: (1) progressive, (2) simple present, (3) future. For each, order the sentences from those judged most correct to those judged least correct. Is this order the same as the order established for the Spanish speakers? If not, how can you account for the difference in relative orderings?

*6. How do you account for the difference in specific percentages for the two language groups?

**7. What do these data suggest about the acquisition of tense/aspect systems in an L2? Is acquisition gradual or is it an all or nothing phenomenon? You might want to compare your answer on this question with that of Problem 4.4 (question 5).

PROBLEM 4.8

(Some knowledge of Spanish is required to do this problem)

Native Language: English
Target Language: Spanish
Background Information: Adolescent
Data Source: Spontaneous utterances

Data

1. Depué cuando *nos* aguantamos por el manos.
   Pero porque *me* mudó aquí ... (= mudé)
2. sí la mamá no *lo* dejó *Raymond* salir ...
3. O caminá-, o* *me* camino o en bicicleta.
   Se vivía en Palmas.
   *es*quedar y *es*quedar. (= se quedaba y se quedaba)
4. ... pregunta a casar con ella.
   Y ella tenía que quedar en el lobby.
   Pue yo quedo con él.
5. ... así pa xxx vender *cosas*.
6. Ello va a llamar *a mí* pa 'cer... que sa fue pa buscar *él*.
   Pero yo no vi *él* mucho.
   Yo sólo visité *la* dos veces.
7. Yo creo que yo *me* gusta menos.
   No *me* gusta ni ...
   No *me* gustaba.
   El no *le* gustaba mucho, ...
   Ella ... que no *me* gustaba ella.
8. El maestro que *me* ensañaba español ...
   ... él *me* contesta en inglés.
   Pue él, ello *me* cambió ...
   No, ello todavía *me* llamaron.
   Cuando *me* llaman.
   A ver si *me* llaman pa pelota.
9. Y la, ell(as) *sa* fueron.
   Pue, todo *sa* fue. ((= se fueron))
   Ella *sa* fue.
   ... que *sa* fue pa buscar él.
   Ella *sa* fue solo a S.F. ...
10. Yo no *me* acuerdo.
    Ya no *me* acuerdo.
    Yo no *me* acuerdo del otro.
    No *me* acuerdo.
11. ... con otro amigo ayudándo*me*
    Y (ellos) no puedo hacer*lo* pa ...
    ... ahí adentro ayudándo*lo*
    ... sí puedamo coger*lo* bien.
    ... no está listo pa casar*se*.
12. El no gustaba *los americanos*.
    Yo gusta *todo* ...
    El no gusta *mucho problema*.
13. pue ponemo en cajas ...
    Ello(s) usaba pa el companía.

Questions

1. Focus on preverbal clitic pronouns. Divide the sentences into two groups, those which are Spanish-like and those which are non-Spanish-like. How is this division related to SVO vs. SOV word order?

2. How does the division in question 1 reflect IL strategies?

3. Focus on the verb *gustar* in 12. What arguments can you make for lexical transfer? You might want to consider subcategorization differences between Spanish and English.

4. Consider sentences with reflexive pronouns. Describe the learner's control of such pronouns.

*5. How would you show that this learner's IL exhibits consistent word order?

PROBLEM 4.9

Native Language: Hebrew
Target Language: English
Background Information: 13 to 15 year-olds
Data Source: Elicited responses in interviews

===== Part I =====

Data

1. I see/**him a year ago.**
2. I saw/**the movie a couple of days ago.**
3. I saw/**him in his apartment.**
4. I study/**in school math science geography gym art.**
5. I like/**English and geography best.**
6. I like/**best Paul Anka Elvis Presley.**
7. I live/**in Forest Park Apartments now.**
8. I lived/**five years ago in Ramat Gan.**
9. You put/**the book in the desk.**
10. You put/**the book on the chair.**
11. I study/**in school mathematics Hebrew.**
12. I met/**him three years ago.**
13. I live/**now at 61 Rambam Street.**
14. I live/**now in Jerusalem.**
15. I live/**now in Ramat Gan.**
16. I live/**5 years ago in Ramat Gan.**
17. I live/**in Jerusalem 5 years ago.**
18. I lived/**in Glenmont Hills a suburb of Wheaton 5 years ago.**
19. I like/**very much movies.**
20. I heard/**them a couple years ago.**
21. I will study/**languages there.**

Questions

1. Focus on the strings in boldface which appear *after the verb* in each IL sentence. State a possible IL generalization to account for the order of elements produced by these learners.

===== Part II =====

Data

Below are additional examples of IL forms produced by these learners:

1. The books are on the table.
2. Yesterday I heard the Beatles.
3. You put the books on the table now.
4. I heard them the last time yesterday.
5. In school I learn English Hebrew.
6. Best I like English and mathematics.
7. Yesterday I saw America America.
8. Now I also live in Ramat Gan.
9. Now I'm living in Tel Aviv.
10. Five years ago I lived in Ramat Gan.
11. One year ago I heard her.
12. In Ramat Gan I saw him.
13. I got it for a present.
14. My father bought it.
15. I saw it two days two days ago.
16. I li- I I lived in Aliya Street.
17. The Israeli singer I like best Rivka Michaeli.
18. The best I like the singer Elvis Presley.
19. I think yesterday I have heard her.
20. One year ago I have I have heard her.

83

Questions

2. How do these additional data complicate the analysis you came up with in Part I?

=== **Part III** ===

Data

The data were elicited by questions of the following type:

A. *What subjects do you study in school?*
I learn geography mathematic mathematic.
I study in school mathematics history geography.
I study at school mathematics Hebrew.
In school I I learn English Hebrew.

I studied at school historia mathematica and sport.
I'm study in school the same subjects.
We learn we learn in school Hebrew mathematics science.

B. *When did you meet your teacher?*
I met Mr. Yanko two years ago.
I meet Nomi three three years ago.
I met him three years ago.
I met Mr. Margaliot two years ago.

I met her at the beginning of the year.
I met her a year before.
I met my mathematics teacher before two years.

C. *Where do you live now?*
I live now at 61 Rambam Street.
Now I live in Jerusalem.
I live in Jerusalem.
I live now in Jerusalem.

Now I'm living in Tel Aviv.
I live now in Ramat Gan.
Now I also live in Ramat Gan.

D. *Where did you live five years ago?*
I lived five years ago in Ramat Gan.
I lived in Tel Aviv.
I lived in Jerusalem five years ago.
I li- I I lived in Aliya Street.

I li- I I lived also in Ramat Gan.
Five years ago I lived in Ramat Gan.
I I have been living in Lud.

E. *Where did you see him?*
I see Mr. Lavon in Ben Yehuda Street.
I saw him in his room.
I saw him in my house.
I saw him in his in his apartment.

I saw him in his office.
I saw him in his house.
In Ramat Gan I saw him.

Questions

**3. It could be claimed that these learners produced answers which reflected the word order of the questions. For example: "What subjects do you *like best*?" produces the response: "I *like best* history." How would you support or refute this claim on the basis of the data presented so far?

**4. What are the methodological implications of continually increasing the data base used in IL analysis?

**5. Describe the fuller corpus given in Appendix I. Produce an analysis of the strings which occur after the verb in each sentence. In light of these additional data, rethink the analysis of questions 1 to 3.

SECTION 5

Spoken and Written Discourse

Many of the concepts dealt with in this section are either linguistic ones or have already been discussed. *Code switching* is introduced in this section for the first time. It refers to the use of two languages within a conversation and deals with the ways in which a speaker switches from one language to another.

Native Language: Arabic
Target Language: English
Background Information: Male, intermediate level of an intensive course program
Data Source: Part I, oral report of a movie entitled "Little Man, Big City"; Part II, written report of the same movie

Part I

Data

I saw today a movie about a man in a big city. I want to tell you about a movie, my friend. The movie began with a man about forty years old or forty-five in his apartment in the city and he was disturbed by alarm clock, TV, and noisy outside the house or outside the apartment and he woke up in a bad temper and he wanted a fresh air, he went when he opened the window to get this fresh air, he found a smoke, smoke air, dirty air. The movie also showed that the man not only disturbed in his special apartment or special house, but in everything, in work, in street, in transportation, even in the gardens and seashores. Man in the city has to wake up very early to go to the work and he has to as the movie shows, he has to use any means of transportation, car, bus, bicycle and all the streets are crowded, and he has no no choice or alternatively to use and he is busy day and night. At day, he has to work hard among the machines, the typewriters and among papers, pencils and offices in the city. And when he wanted to take a rest in his house or outside his house in the garden or the seashore. . . . He can't because the seats are crowded with people. When he wanted to take a meal in restaurant, the restaurant is crowded, everything is crowded in the city and very, very—it's not good place or good atmosphere to to live in. The movie showed that. And the man began to feel sick and thus he wanted to consult the doctors to describe a medicine or anything for for health, but the doctors also disagreed about his illness or they couldn't diagnose his illness correctly. This they show at first. Want to make us know about the life in the city. The man began to think about to find a solution or answer for this dilemma. OK dilemma? Dilemma. He thought that why not to go to the open lands and to build houses and gardens and and to live in this new fresh land with fresh air and fresh atmosphere and why don't we stop smoking in the factories by using filters, filters and stop smoking from the cars and all industrial bad survivals or like smoking like dirty airs and so on. The man also wanted to make kids or childrens in the houses not to play or to use sports inside houses, but to go outside the houses in the garden and to play with balls, basket anything. They like to play. And also he wanted to live in a quiet and calm apartment. People inside houses must not use TV in a bad way or a noisy way. Must use it in a calm way or in a quiet way and that, I think, that is a good solution or a good answer for this city dilemma.

Questions

1. Categorize the data by separating this speaker's use of the present tense from his use of the past tense. Continue the model format as set up below:

Past	*Present*
I saw today a movie about a man in a big city.	
	I want to tell you about a movie, my friend.
The movie began with a man about forty years old or forty-five in his apartment in the city and he was disturbed by alarm clock, TV, . . .	

2. Focusing on tense shifts, from past to present and vice versa, work out an IL generalization which might account for this shift.

=== **Part II** ===

Data

I saw a movie about a man in a city (big city). I want to tell you what I saw and what is my opinion. The movie began with a man about forty years old, in his apartment in a big city. He was disturbed by many things like Alarm O'Clock, T.V., Radio and noisy outside. He want a fresh air, but he could not because the city is not a good place for fresh air. There are many factories which fill the air with smoke. The movie showed the daily life of a man in the city. He is very busy day and night. He had to go to his work early by any means of transportation, car, bus, bicycle. The streets are crowded, everything in the city is crowded with people, the houses, streets, factories, institutions and even the seashores. Man in a big city lives a hard and unhealthy life, noisy, dirt air, crowded houses and smoke are good factors for sickness. The man in the big city tried to find answer to this dilemma. Instead of living in crowded, unhealthy places, he wanted places that must be used for living. People must live in good atmosphere climate and land. Gardens, which are good places for sports, must surround houses. My opinion is that man's solution for the problem is good and acceptable especially for health.

Questions

3. Categorize the data by separating this speaker's use of the present tense from his use of the past tense, as in Part I:

Past   *Present*

4. Focusing on tense shifts, from past to present and vice versa, work out an IL generalization which might account for this shift.

*5. Account for the similarities/differences between this Arabic learner's tense shifting in written discourse as opposed to the oral version. Provide examples detailing your explanation. (In formulating an answer to this question, you may wish to refer back to the comparison of the spoken and written data in Problem 2.1.)

PROBLEM 5.2

Native Language: Italian
Target Language: English
Background Information: Male intermediate level in an intensive ESL program
Data Source: Part I, oral report of a movie entitled "Little Man, Big City"; Part II, written report of the same movie

===== Part I =====

Data

So it there was a movie, um probably filmed some years ago in Budapest . . . from . . . it was a Hungarian? a Hungarian film. It was a cartoon, and it dealt with modern life in the big city. The man who uh well the. . . . It is a description of the life of a man in a big city. From morning when he wakes up and go to work with many other people all living in the same . . . under the same circumstances and uh with the same paternistic form in the big city. And from a very common description of life of modern life, of our pressure, of our stress, of our anxieties and of all the um possible uh limits and uh rules we have to follow living in a big city. And it deals with uh it dealt with pollution problems in a town, in a city where industry and uh residential areas are very close together. And. . . the moral of the story is uh that if people could do something all together the population would have the courage and the will to do eh something for . . . to deal with these problems that may reasonably be able to find a solution or to encourage authorities to face the problem and . . . to find solutions to the . . . to it, because it's not so difficult in fact.

Questions

1. Categorize the data by separating this speaker's use of the present tense from his use of the past tense. Follow the format set up in Problem 5.1.

2. Focusing on tense shifts, from past to present and vice versa, work out an IL generalization which might account for this shift.

===== Part II =====

Data

The film dealt mainly with problems concerning our modern life in a big city. The main character of the story is an ordinary man living and working in the city. The film describes his everyday life and shows him in the different moments of a typical working day. In doing this the author of the story tell us about general very common problems of a modern city, where "civilization," industrialization and the consequent need for more apartament buildings, have brought to serious damages to the environment. A city, therefore, where people do not live, but vegetate; where it is hard to find peace and loneliness; where pollution constantly endangers our health. Towards the end, however, the author suggests the possibility of finding solutions and bringing improvements to the present condition through the active participation of citizens in dealing with the matter.

Questions

3. Categorize the data by separating this speaker's use of the present tense from his use of the past tense, as in Part I.

4. Focusing on tense shifts, from past to present and vice versa, work out an IL generalization which might account for this shift.

*5. Account for the similarities/differences between this learner's tense shifting in written discourse as opposed to the oral version. Provide examples detailing your explanation.

**6. What similarities/differences do you find between the Arabic speaker's description of the film (both oral and written) in Problem 5.1 and the Italian speaker's description of the same film?

PROBLEM 5.3

Native Languages: Apache and Navajo
Target Language: English
Background Information: Adult university students
Data Source: Part I, oral story (Apache); Part II, written composition (Navajo); Part III, written compositions and letters (1,745) (Navajo)

Information about Apache and Navajo: Apache and Navajo are languages closely related in form and have similar rhetorical conventions.

======= Part I =======

Data

English translation of an Apache text

And in 1944 her father and her mother and my wife's father, he works in Miami. And she has been married to me for 25 years. And two months ago she was up there with this other man; the man works at the tribal office; that's where he works. And my wife, and my wife, and she visits with him; she tells me. And me I work here over at the copper mine. And I tell them my wife is no good. And my wife is no good. I don't understand. I don't know why. And this man, and this man, and this man, he works over at the tribal office. And my wife and these two go to Globe, and they visit the bar and tavern. And they were sitting in there, and I talked to them last Thursday when I was in there. And I talked to them.

Questions

1. In Apache, repetition is a valued stylistic rhetorical strategy described by some as conveying emphasis. Based on these data, how would you define repetition?

======= Part II =======

Data

To have a family is a great thing that could happen to a woman. She will also be loved and respected by her children when they all grow up and when she gets old. She won't be alone all the time. They respect her with great pride for raising them and she will not be neglected. And she will not suffer loneliness. The woman will be in great need of someone who loves her. She will be neglected by other people and will be left alone with things and hard work, that she can't do by herself. She will want somebody to turn to for help. The hard work will make her ill and put her in a bad health condition, if she do the hard work or if it worries her. She will be in great need of someone who loves her. She will be alone and will want some company from a person. . . .

Questions

2. How would you quantify the amount of repetition in this English composition written by a Navajo student?

3. How does his use of repetition reflect Navajo/Apache NL use of repetition?

*4. What evidence is there for transfer of the rhetorical strategy of repetition?

======= **Part III** =======

Data

A. livestock
    alone
    help
    ceremony
    family

B. money
    gamble
    steal

C. actor(s)
    movies

Questions

*5. In the English compositions of Navajo students, there is a greater frequency of repetition of words in order from Category A to Category B and from Category B to Category C. What differences are there in these three groups of words which might account for the difference in frequency?

*6. How is the rhetorical strategy of repetition in these L2 data dependent on the semantics of the topic?

PROBLEM 5.4

Native Language: Chichewa
Target Language: English
Background Information: Grade 10 student
Data Source: Written composition

Part I

Data

A Friend

I have the best of all my friends at this school. He is a boy of seventeen. We came to know each other in the first term of the first year. He is also a second former as I am.

This friend of mine has a round smooth face, small and sparkling eyes with arched eye-brows. His mouth is upturned with thick lips and has white clean teeth. He has big nose, big ears, small chin, expanded cheeks and very short black curly hair. His body build is of normal shape with broad shoulders. He is light in complexion and the whole body is covered with fur. He is short, stout and bow-legged.

For all the descriptions, this friend is fit to be a football player or a boxer because of his big, strong muscles. He often smiles and sometimes frowns when annoyed.

Questions

1. Consider this pupil's use of anaphora (the use of one expression which has the same referent as another, e.g., I dropped the glass and then *it* broke). Describe any errors in terms of target language norms of commission and omission.

Part II

Data

It's high time men ceased to regard women as second-class citizens

It is true that men and women are basically equal but it depends on what type of man or woman we mean because in some cases a woman may be found more responsible than a man while in some other cases weaker and the same applies to a man as well.

We can now see that men and women are granted the same responsibilities and it is even proved that women are superior to men in every field. However, men are clever because they claimed to do most complicated jobs in the world leaving the simpler to women. They refuse to acknowledge women's ability due to the fact that they are quite as good as men and that they can do better than they do; therefore it is a man's duty to discourage men from being superior to men by offering them lighter jobs and convincing them that they are delicate creatures so that they shouldn't work as hard as a man. They are always afraid of being beaten in every field, knowing that if women were given a chance of proving their ability in every field, they would certainly succeed.

In some other jobs like driving, it is the women who are responsible drivers. They cause fewer accidents on the road than men do. On the other hand men are capable of understanding things and react quickly and also solving acute problems. Men are active, in most cases they are strong and they can withstand pressure of any sort. Women are looked upon every now and again due to some weaknesses found in them and that is why they are overruled by men and being directed to do their wishes and household work. But this is not to say that they are supposed to be housewives throughout their lives, but they are being reasonable knowing that bearing and rearing children are the most important jobs. Of course this is a fundamental idea in a human life because without their care we would definitely perish right away from the beginning.

Women are good peace makers that even negociations by them always proves a success due to their sweet tongues and beautiful body structure which attracts men to reveal their secrets. Some things are too important to be done by men therefore they are done adequately by women. Some of them are quite sympathetic to let men look after important affairs and that is why there are few women in politics. They are not excluded but they exclude themselves as being polite to men.

Women are short-tempered, unreliable, irrational; therefore cannot do certain jobs like top-level political negotiation, banking and no vote in certain countries. They are not trusted. They leave their jobs to get married.

However, women are not to be looked down upon by men due to the fact that we are all human beings and the only difference being that each one has a part to play in a family.

Questions

2. This composition was written by the same pupil 18 months later. Consider his use of anaphora at this time. Describe any errors in terms of target language norms of commission and omission.

3. Compare these two compositions. What differences/similarities do you notice between them in terms of the English system of reference? Does the second one seem to show any "improvement" over the first one? If so, in what ways?

*4. Consider the two compositions (both individually and comparatively) from the point of view of this pupil's use of conjunctions (e.g., *and, but*).

Native Language: Chichewa/English bilingual
Background Information: Bilingual child, 2 years 4 months
Data Source: Spontaneous speech

Part I

Data

Transcript I

Parents' Utterances to Child (D = father; M = mother)

Child's Utterances (child aged 2 years 4 months)

is it hot, dolly?/dolly, is it hot?/is it hot?/is it hot?/
it's ... it's hot/the water's hot, daddy/

D: Ufuna tithire madzi ena, tiziziritse?
(You-want we-put water other, we-make-cold?)
(Do you want us to add more water to make it cold?)

uziziritse/
(you-make-cold)
(make it cold)

D: Eh?

uthire ... uziziritse madzi otentha/
(you-put you-make-cold water hot)
(add ... make the hot water cold)

D: Madzi otentha a chiani?
(Water hot of what?)
(What is the hot water for?)

Ona Christopher, wasamba.
(See Christopher, he-has-bathed)
(Look at Christopher, he has had a bath)

(M. puts cold water into doll's bath)

M: Ona, ndathira madzi ozizira. Ndaziziritsa.
(See, I-have-put water cold. I-have-made-cold)
(Look, I have added cold water. I have made it cold)

ndikusambitsa dolly/ndifuna sopo wa dolly/
(I-am-bathing dolly/I-want soap of dolly)
(I am bathing dolly/I want some soap for dolly)

D: Ufuna sopo wa dolly?
(You-want soap of dolly?)
(Do you want some soap for dolly?)

(D. gives child some soap)

D: Eh.

oh, dolly's soap/

D: Sunena zikomo? Em?
(Not-you-will-say thank-you? Em?)
(Won't you say thank you? Em?)

Tina, umati chiani?
Tina, you-say what?)
Tina, what do you say?)

zikomo/
(thank-you)

D: Eh-eh.

(child whispers to herself while bathing doll)

D: Ukuchita chiani, Tina? Eh?
(You-are-doing what, Tina? Eh?)
(What are you doing, Tina? Eh?)

nkikum'sambitsa dolly/
(I-am-her-bathing dolly)
(I am bathing dolly)

D: Dolly akulira?
(Dolly she-is-crying?)
(Is dolly crying?)

akusamba, sakulira/
(she-is-bathing, not-she-is-crying)
(she is having a bath, she is not crying)

95

Parents' Utterances to Child (D = father; M = mother)	Child's Utterances (child aged 2 years 4 months)

Parents' Utterances to Child (D = father; M = mother)

D: Sakulira?   Osam'nyamula   bwanji?
(Not-she-is-crying? You-not-her-carry how?)
(She isn't crying? Why don't you carry her?)

   Um'nyamule, um'sambitse miyendo.
   You-her-carry, you-her-bathe legs.
   Hold her,   wash her legs.

   Umuike   m'bafa pang'ono
   You-her-put in-bath little)
(Don't drown her.)

D: You haven't finished washing . . . bathing her, have you?

D: Why do you want a towel for dolly?

D: Why do you want it?

D: Ufuna   uchite   naye   chiani?
(You-want you-do with-her what?)
(What do you want to do with her?)

D: Me?

D: You want me to go and sleep?

D: Ufuna   towel wa chiani? Ufuna   uchite
(You-want towel of what? You-want you-do
(What do you want a towel for? What do you

   naye   chiani?
   with-her what?
   want to do with her?)

D: Ufuna   madzi otentha kapena ozizira?
(You-want water hot   or   cold?)
(Do you want hot water or cold?)

D: Ufuna   madzi otentha ndi ozizira?
(You-want water hot   with cold?)
(Do you want hot water with the cold?)

D: Have you finished wiping your boots?

D: Who's a girl?

D: What's her name?

D: Her name is Dolly, is it?

D: Who gave her that name?

D: You've finished to wipe the cloth?

D: Thank you.

D: She's a what?

D: She's a dry now, is she?

Child's Utterances (child aged 2 years 4 months)

I want a towel for dolly/I want a towel for dolly/

dolly want to take a towel/dolly . . . /

I want a towel for daddy for dolly/
(i.e., *from* daddy)

dolly want a towel/

daddy, go away/go and sleep/sleep/

sleep/

no, I want dolly to sleep/

uthire   madzi otentha m'madzi ozizira/
(you-put water hot   in-water cold)
(add hot water to the cold water)

ndifuna madzi otentha m'ozizira madzi/
(I-want   water hot   in-cold   water)
(I want hot water in the cold water)

yeah'it's O.K./
dolly/oh, dolly, you're a girl/you're a girl/
.
.
.
daddy, come and take a cloth, come and take a cloth/

I've finished to wiping your boots/dolly . . . big/she's a girl/

dolly is a girl/

Dolly/

her name is Dolly/

dolly, I stop you/stop/you . . . you spill the water, dolly/I want to push you/I've finished to wipe the dolly/take my cloth/

I've finished to wipe the cloth/take it/

dolly is a all dry/

she's dry/she's dry/

Parents' Utterances to Child (D = father; M = mother)	*Child's Utterances (child aged 2 years 4 months)*
	she's dry now/
D: Oh, that's fine. That's fine.	
	⋮
M: Tina, have you finished bathing dolly now? Did you finish bathing dolly?	
	dolly spill a water/
M: Eh-eh. You wipe it up then. Tina, it's time for you to have a bath now.	
	oh, dolly want to have a bath/
M: All right, you leave dolly in her bath, and Tina come and have her bath. You come and have your bath now, Tina. Up you get.	
	I've finished to wipe it/
M: Thank you. Up you get.	(child crying)
M: Come on. Stand up.	
	I can't stand up/
M: You hold on to mummy's legs. Come on. Of course you can stand up.	
	I can't stand up/
M: Come on. Hold mummy's hand.	no/
M: Come on. Hold my hands.	no/
	(child finally gets up)
M: Oh. Up you get. Now. Masula mabatoni.	
(Undo buttons)	
(Undo your buttons)	
(M. undoes cardigan buttons)	oh, no, I don't . . ./
	(child cries)
	no, don't take my buttons off/no, don't take it off/
M: I'm not taking your buttons off. I'm undoing them.	
	don't doing them/no, you're a naughty/
(M. and D. laugh)	
M: Bvula pinafore, Tina.	
(Take-off pinafore, Tina.	
(Take off your pinafore, Tina)	
	sindifuna kubvula pinafore/
	(not-I-want to-take-off pinafore)
	(I don't want to take off my pinafore)
D: Tsopano usamba bwanji?	
(Now you-will-bath how?)	
(So how will you have a bath?)	
	no/no/ (screaming)
M: Come on.	

Questions

1. Identify instances of code switching in this child's speech.

2. Identify errors in terms of the TL norms of English. Do these errors appear to be developmentally based or NL-based? Provide evidence to support your claims.

Data

Transcript 2

Mother's Utterances to Child

Ufuna   kumina?
(You-want to-blow?)
(Do you want to blow your nose?)

Child's Utterances (child aged 2 years 6 months)

kumina/
(to-blow)
(to blow my nose)

Dikira ndikatenge mpango.
(Wait I-go-take   handkerchief)
(Wait for me to get a handkerchief)

I'm sore on my leg/

Eh?

my sore leg/

(M. wiping her nose)

I can't blow my nose/

Sungathe   kumina? Chifukwa?
(Not-you-can to-blow? Why?)
(Can't you blow your nose? Why not?)

my . . . I'm sore, mummy/I'm sore/

Ukumva   kuphweteka pati?
(You-feel to-hurt   on-what?)
(Where do you feel sore?)

pa min . . . /pa knee . . . mimi/
(on mim . . . /on knee . . . mimi)
(child struggling to find Chichewa word for "knee")

Ukumva   kuphweteka pati?
(You-feel to-hurt   on-what?)
(Where do you feel sore?)

pa knee/pa knee/pa knee/pa knee/
(on knee)
(on my knee)

Pa   mawondo.
(On knees)
(On your knees)

pa wamwondo/
(on wamwondo)
(child struggling to imitate "mawondo" = "knees")

Mawondo.
(Knees)

mawondo/
(knees)

mummy, I want to sleep on you/

Iai,   ndifuna kuluka.
(No, I-want   to knit)
(No, I want to knit)

mummy, I want to sleep on the . . . /mummy/

Kagone   pa bedi.
(Go-sleep on bed)
(Go and sleep on the bed)

eh-eh/

Sufuna?   Ufuna   kupanga chiani?
(Not-you-want? You-want to-do   what?)
(Don't you want to? What do you want to do?)

kugona, oh . . . eh-eh, pa . . . pa book/
(to-sleep, oh . . . eh-eh (=no), on . . . on book)
(to sleep, oh . . . eh-eh, on . . . on the book)

Eh?

pa book/
(on book)
(on the book)

Pa   book chiani?
(On book what?)
(What do you mean "on the book"?)

Mother's Utterances to Child	*Child's Utterances (child aged 2 years 6 months)*
	pa book wa daddy/
	(on book of daddy)
	(on daddy's book)
Ufuna kugona pa mabuku?	
(You-want to-sleep on books?)	
(Do you want to sleep on the books?)	
	eee/
	(yes)
Chifukwa?	
(Why?)	
	it's a naughty book/another book/
It's a naughty book, is it? Why is it naughty? Eh?	
Why is it naughty?	real mess on the book/
Eh?	
There's a mess on the book, is there?	yes/
Waipitsa ndani?	
(He/she-made-dirty who?)	
(Who messed it up?)	waipitsa Kadama bukhu/
	(she-made-dirty Kadama book)
	(Kadama messed the book)
Eh-eh! (M. laughs)	
	bukhu wa mama/
	(book of mummy)
	(mummy's book)
Iai. Ndimaganiza kuti Tina waipitsa.	
(No. I-was-thinking that Tina she-made-dirty)	
(No. I thought it was Tina who messed it up)	em/ waipitsa bukhu/
	(em/ she-made-dirty book)
	(em/she messed the book)
Ndani?	
(Who?)	Tina waipitsa bukhu/
	(Tina she-made-dirty book)
	(Tina messed the book)
Waipitsa bwanji?	
(She-made-dirty how?)	Tina is a naughty girl/
(Why did you mess it up?)	
	Tina's a very good girl/
Eh-eh!	
(M. laughs)	
Ukupanga chiani ndi zala?	
(You-are-doing what with fingers?)	
(What are you doing with your toes?)	
	zala iyi/
	(fingers this)
	(this toes)
Zala izi.	
(Fingers these)	
(These toes)	zala izi/
	(fingers these)
	(these toes)
Ndi zala izi. Zala za mapazi.	
(Is/are fingers these. Fingers of feet)	zala/
(These are toes. Toes)	(fingers)
Zala za manja.	
(Fingers of hands)	
(Fingers)	zala ya . . ./
	(fingers of (singular) . . .)
Za.	
(Of (plural))	

Mother's Utterances to Child	Child's Utterances (child aged 2 years 6 months)
	za manja/ (of hands)
Eee. (Yes)	
	zala ya .../ (fingers of (singular) ...)
Za. (Of (plural))	
	za mpando wa mama/ (of chair of mummy) (of mummy's chair)
(M. laughs) Zala za mpando! (Fingers of chair!)	
	zala za .../ (fingers of ...)
Iai, mikono. (No, arms)	
	mikono wa Tina/ (arms of (singular) Tina) (Tina's arms)
Mikono. (arms)	
	mikono wa Tina/ (arms of (singular) Tina) (Tina's arms)
Ya Tina. (Of (plural) Tina)	
	ya daddy/ (of daddy)
Mikono ya daddy. (Arms of daddy) (Daddy's arms)	
	ya... mikono ya mama ndi mikono (of... arms of (plural) mummy and arms wa... of (singular)) (of... mummy's arms and ?'s arms)
Mikono. (Arms)	
	mikono wa Tina/ (arms of (singular) Tina) (Tina's arms)
Ya Tina. (Of (plural) Tina)	
	ya daddy/ya mummy/ (of daddy/of mummy) (daddy's/mummy's)
Eh-eh.	ya mama/ ya Tina/ (of mummy/ of Tina) (mummy's/Tina's)
Eh-eh.	and my shoes . . . /
Eh-eh.	for Farida and for Tina/these ones/
They're like Farida's, aren't they?	like Farida's/they're for Tina/they're for . . .
They're Tina's shoes.	they're Farida's shoes/
No. Those aren't Farida's shoes. Those are Tina's shoes, but they're like Farida's shoes.	like Farida's shoes/
Eh-eh.	

Questions

3. The child in this transcript is the same child as in Part I, but two months later. At this time the child was dominant in English. What evidence is there that this child is "losing" her first language, Chichewa?

*4. Which aspects of Chichewa does she seem to have difficulty remembering? Support your conclusions with specific examples.

**5. Compare the two transcripts. What similarities/differences do you find between these two time periods?

PROBLEM 5.6

Native Language: Tatar
Target Language: Russian
Background Information: Two schoolchildren
Data Source: Picture description (translation)

Data

Child 1 / Written in NL (Tatar)

The long awaited spring has come. The days are getting warmer and warmer. The blue sky is covered by white fluffy clouds. They skim like sailboats through the sky. The ice is breaking away on the river to the north. The birds have returned after having flown from us to a warm region. The apples have bloomed. Children are planting tomatoes, cucumbers, onions and other vegetables. They are watering the trees. Azat is planting flowers. Rustam is watering the apples. The children are happily working in the garden. They are very happy.

Written in TL (Russian)

In the schoolyard there is a large garden. Children are digging in the earth. Children are working in the garden. In the garden there is a pine tree, an oak, and tomatoes. An apple tree is growing there. They are planting flower beds.

Child 2 / Written in NL (Tatar)

It was a beautiful spring day. The sun was shining. The birds who had returned from distant lands were singing. The trees were swallowed up by the greenery of the luxuriant spring foliage. The children have come into their garden. There the apple trees have already blossomed. Rustam is watering the flowers. The remaining children are planting vegetables. The teacher is watching the work of her pupils. She's pleased with their work, she smiles.

Written in TL (Russian)

In the schoolyard there is a large garden. Children are working there. The garden is big. In the garden there are trees. A child is planting a tree. A child is pouring water from a watering pot. In the garden a poplar is growing.

Questions

1. What kind of information (e.g., descriptive, evaluative, etc.) do these children include in their TL description of these pictures?

2. What kind of information do these children include in their NL description of these pictures?

3. What similarities/differences do you see between NL and TL versions of these pictures?

*4. Are the similarities/differences the same for both children?

PROBLEM 5.7

(Some knowledge of French is required to do this problem)

Native Language: English
Target Language: French
Background Information: There are five groups, three nonnative (NN) and two native (N):
    A.   grade 1 early total immersion (100% schooling in French), total = 1000 hours;
    B.   grade 9/10 late immersion (exposed to French 20 to 30 minutes per day in grades 6 and 7; 55 to 70 percent immersion in grade 8; 25 to 40 percent in grades 9 and 10), total = 1000 hours;
    C.   grade 9/10 early partial immersion (exposure to French 1/2 day since grade 1);
    D.   grade 1 native French speaking children;
    E.   grade 9/10 native French speaking children
Data Source: Responses to questions about cartoon drawings

Data

Question: Imagine maintenant que tu rencontres ce monsieur dans la rue et que tu veux savoir quelle heure il est. Alors, qu'est-ce que tu lui dis? Tu veux être très poli, n'est-ce pas, parce que tu ne le connais pas. Alors, moi, je fais le monsieur. Qu'est-ce que tu dis au monsieur?

Student Response:

A. Early immersion—grade 1

Student	Response
1	Bonjour, monsieur, est-ce que tu as le temps?
2	Quelle heure il est, monsieur?
3	Quelle heure il est?
4	um . . . je vais um /di/ à toi quel /trwa/ temps il est.
5	Quand est-ce que tu as réveillé? . . . Est-ce que tu es très fatigué? . . . Est-ce que tu veux aller dormir un autre fois ou va faire ton travail?
6	Quelle heure tu es? . . . s'il vous plaît.
7	J'ai pas un montre
8	/ɛle/ toi /e/ le temps s-sur le main?
9	Bonjour. Comment ça va? Ça va bien merci. Eum . . . est-ce que tu veux un bonbon? (*laughs*)
10	Je dis: /mɔs/—excuse-moi, monsieur. Quelle heure est-ce qu'il est?
11	Excusez-moi, est-ce que tu as l'heure?
12	Est-ce que tu as une eum une—(qu'est-ce que) c'est c'est encore—une montre? Quelle heure est-ce que c'est?

B. Grade 9/10 late immersion

Student	Response
1	um um pardonne-moi, monsieur, mais uh je ne pas un uh manteau, et est-ce que je peux uh demander quelle heure est-il?
2	un pardon, m-monsieur. Je n'ai pas—'or' je—quelle est—quelle heure est-il?
3	Pardon, monsieur, uh est-ce vous avez le—l'heure?
4	um . . . uh s'il vous plaît, quelle heure est-il, excusez-moi.
5	uh excusez-moi, monsieur. Euh est-ce que vous savez quelle heure est-il?
6	Il—il veut savoir uh—Oh uh O.K. uh quelle heure est-il?
7	Vous êtes un monsieur? (*laughs*) Euh, pardonnez-moi, monsieur, Est-ce que vous pouvez me dire le temps—le temps?
8	uh bonjour uh . . . je ne sais pas uh . . . uh pas très bien uh . . . après je dis uh "bonjour" je peux um dis uh "quelle heure est-il?" Et uh quand uh il me donne le l'heure uh je partis.

9	Oh uh je parl/e/ avec ce monsieur et—Vous uh et uh je pos/e/ la question: "quelle temps est-il?" et um—
10	A quelle heure est-ce que tu (*laughs*) as um réveillé ce matin? Oh je je dis: "Bonjour, monsieur. Quelle heure il est?"
11	uh je dis que il umm, non. Je—je prends la question: quelle heure est-ce que tu um all/e/ au lit? (*lengthy discussion of merits of early bed-going*) Oh! Je demande quelle heure est-il?
12	xxx /ke/—quelle heure il est? Oh umm pardon, monsieur, um . . . (*laughs*) umm, pouvez-vous me—me /di/ quelle heure /ilel/ s- quelle heure il est, s'il vous plaît?

C. Grade 9/10 early partial immersion

Student	Response
1	Excuse-moi, mais as-tu l'heure? (*laughs*)
2	um excusez-moi, monsieur, est-ce que tu oh as le temps non—tu /tra/ le temps?
3	Excuse-moi, monsieur. Avez-vous le temps? Quelle heure est-il?
4	mm . . . hm . . . je demande le temps de—de sa temps. O.K. um pardon, monsieur, est-ce que tu peux me /do/—me /di/ le temps? What time is it?
5	quelle heure est-il? Euh mm
6	Je dis: "Excusez-moi, /məsər/ monsieur, est-ce que tu peux me dire quelle heure est-il?" et il va me dire et je dis: "Merci beaucoup," et puis je pars. (*laughs*)
7	Oh je le dire: "Monsieur, euh je m'excuse, mais est-ce que tu as le temps, s'il vous plaît?"
8	um, excuse-moi, monsieur, um mais je n'ai pas une montre et je veux savoir quel est le temps? Et um et puis quand il a le dit et je dis merci.
9	O.K. Je lui dis: "Excuse-moi, monsieur!. umm, est-ce que p—tu peux /di/ moi quelle heure est-il?"
10	um bonjour, monsieur. Uh excusez-moi, est-ce que tu peux me dire quelle heure est-il?
11	eum je lui demande s'il y a un montre et si il n'y a pas je peux pas lui demander, mais s'il a, je demande le temps—quelle heure est. um je dis: "monsieur, est-ce que tu sais l'heure maintenant?" Et il me dit: "c'est onze heures et demie," et je dis: "Oh, merci beaucoup."
12	umm excuse-moi, monsieur. Quelle heure est-il?

D. Grade 1 native French speaking children

Student	Response
1	Quelle heure est-il?
2	Je dis: "Quelle heure il est, monsieur?" Il me répond.
3	S'il vous plaît, est-ce que je pourrais savoir l'heure?
4	Oui, ben je dis: "Il est quelle heure?"
5	Est-ce que je peux savoir l'heure, s'il vous plaît?
6	J'y dis: /ke/—est-ce que vous pourrez me di- est-ce que vous pourriez me dire il est quelle heure?
7	Quelle heure qu'il est?
8	Monsieur, s'il vous plaît, quelle heure est-il?
9	Euh . . . voulez-vous me dire quelle heure il est?
10	Je dis: "Monsieur, est-ce que vous voulez me dire il est quelle heure?"
11	Je dis: "Monsieur, est-ce que euh est-ce que vous pouvez me dire l'heure, s'il vous plaît?"
12	. . . Je sais pas . . . L'heure (*laughs*) . . . Je sais p- . . .

E. Grade 9/10 native French speaking children

Student	Response
1	Oh ben, excusez-moi, monsieur, euh est-ce que vous auriez l'heure, s'il vous plaît?
2	Je dis euh: "Excusez-moi, est-ce que vous avez l'heure, s'il vous plaît?"
3	Ben, je m'excuse de vous déranger. Est-ce que je pourrais savoir l'heure, s'il vous plaît?
4	Ah oui. Pardon, monsieur. Avez-vous l'heure?
5	Pardon monsieur. Est-ce que vous auriez l'heure, par hasard?

6	Je dis: "Excusez, monsieur!" Là là il va se retourner, je dis: "Est-ce que je pourrais avoir l'heure, s'il vous plaît?
8	Euh excusez-moi, monsieur. Auriez-vous l'heure?
9	Excusez-moi, monsieur, mais est-ce que vous avez l'heure?
10	Ah ben excusez-moi, monsieur. Pourriez-vous me dire l'heure, s'il vous plaît?
11	Auriez-vous l'heure, s'il vous plaît?
12	Excusez-moi, est-ce que vous avez l'heure, s'il vous plaît?

Questions

1. Focus on the use of politeness forms (e.g., *vous, excusez-moi, monsieur*). Categorize each of the five groups according to the ways in which the students express politeness.

2. How do the grade 1 NSs (Category D) differ from the grade 9/10 NSs (Category E)? In what ways are they similar?

3. What are the similarities/differences among the three immersion groups?

*4. What conclusions can you draw about the differences between NSs and NNSs in their use of politeness in French? Consider the differences from the point of view of a single point in time (i.e., grade 1 NS vs. grade 1 NNS) and as a function of exposure to French (i.e., early total immersion vs. late immersion vs. early partial immersion).

PROBLEM 5.8

Native Languages: English and Russian
Target Language: Hebrew
Background Information: Adult university students
Data Source: Oral responses to eight different situations

Data

Situation 1

You are at a meeting and you say something that one of the participants interprets as a personal insult to him:

> *He:* I feel that your last remark was directed at me and I take offense.
> *You:* . . . .

Situation 2

You completely forget a crucial meeting at the office with your boss. An hour later you call him to apologize. The problem is that this is the second time you've forgotten such a meeting. Your boss gets on the line and asks:

> *Boss:* What happened to you?
> *You:* . . . .

Situation 3

You forget a get-together with a friend. You call him to apologize. This is already the second time you've forgotten such a meeting. Your friend asks over the phone:

> *Friend:* What happened?
> *You:* . . . .

Situation 4

You call from work to find out how things are at home and your son reminds you that you forgot to take him shopping, as you had promised, and this is the second time that this has happened. Your son says over the phone:

> *Son:* Oh, you forgot again and you promised!
> *You:* . . . .

Situation 5

Backing out of a parking place, you run into the side of another car. It was clearly your fault. You dent in the side door slightly. The driver gets out and comes over to you angrily.

> *Driver:* Can't you look where you're going? See what you've done!
> *You:* . . . .

Situation 6

You accidentally bump into a well-dressed elderly lady at an elegant department store, causing her to spill her packages all over the floor. You hurt her leg, too. It's clearly your fault and you want to apologize profusely.

> *She:* Ow, my goodness!
> *You:* . . . .

Situation 7

You bump into a well-dressed lady at a department store, shaking her up a bit. It's your fault, and you want to apologize.

> *She:* Hey, look out!
> *You:* . . . .

Situation 8

You bump into an elderly lady at a department store. You hardly could have avoided doing it because she was blocking the way. Still you feel that some kind of apology is in order.

> *She:* Oh, my!
> *You:* . . . .

The following response types were observed:

Type	Example
Apology	I'm sorry.
Explanation	There was a terrible traffic jam.
Responsibility	It was my fault. I didn't see you.
Repair	I'll repay you.
Promise of forbearance	I'll make sure it won't happen again.

For the various response types, the following results obtained for each of the eight situations.

Percentage of Responses

	NLs			ILs	
	NE	NR	NH	E in H	R in H
Situation 1:					
Apology	92	66	66	69	64
Explanation	42	33	33	23	21
Responsibility	100	75	58	92	71
Repair	0	0	8	0	0
Forbearance	0	0	0	0	7
Situation 2:					
Apology	75	66	66	61	64
Explanation	100	50	92	77	70
Responsibility	50	66	16	77	100
Repair	42	0	0	0	14
Forbearance	25	33	16	23	64
Situation 3:					
Apology	75	42	58	38	57
Explanation	100	100	92	100	100
Responsibility	75	92	50	77	100
Repair	33	8	25	8	21
Forbearance	0	8	8	0	57
Situation 4:					
Apology	67	33	50	54	38
Explanation	92	17	50	38	46
Responsibility	33	50	0	46	64
Repair	92	25	66	46	43
Forbearance	42	66	16	23	71
Situation 5:					
Apology	67	50	58	69	64
Explanation	50	8	25	38	43
Responsibility	58	33	66	62	64
Repair	66	75	75	78	86
Forbearance	0	0	0	8	0
Situation 6:					
Apology	92	100	83	100	86
Explanation	16	0	0	16	7
Responsibility	33	16	0	30	14
Repair	100	42	100	69	43
Forbearance	8	0	0	0	7
Situation 7:					
Apology	83	100	92	92	86
Explanation	25	0	16	31	21
Responsibility	58	25	42	46	57
Repair	25	0	17	8	0
Forbearance	8	0	0	0	7

	NLs			ILs	
	NE	NR	NH	E in H	R in H
Situation 8:					
Apology	92	100	33	92	100
Explanation	42	16	75	31	36
Responsibility	8	0	16	23	14
Repair	8	0	0	8	0
Forbearance	0	0	0	0	0

NE = native English, n =12   E in H = native English in Hebrew,
NR = native Russian, n = 12 n = 13
NH = native Hebrew, n = 12   R in H = native Russian in Hebrew,
                                     n = 14

Questions

1. Do the types of apologies used differ for the three groups of native speakers? If so, how?

2. Consider each situation separately. Do the apologies in Hebrew of L1 English and L1 Russian speakers reflect NL patterns? If so, how?

3. If the answer to 2 is no, how might you account for the difference?

4. Given the overall pattern of apologies, does the pattern of apologies in the NL and the IL differ?

5. If you find differences in question 4, how do you account for them?

*6. Are the patterns the same or different for the IL behavior of Russian and English native speakers?

*7. If there are differences, to what do you attribute them?

SECTION 6

Foreigner Talk Discourse

The problems in this section come primarily from the literature on conversations involving NNSs. Concepts which may be helpful are:

1. Foreigner talk
2. Foreigner talk discourse
3. Negotiation of meaning
4. Modified input
5. Modified interaction

Foreigner talk refers to the language used by NSs of a language when addressing a NNS.

Foreigner talk discourse refers to the area of inquiry involving NNSs in conversation.

Negotiation of meaning involves aspects of conversation which are devoted to mutual understanding by the participants.

Modified input refers to the speech modifications which NSs make in addressing NNSs.

In addition to modifications in the speech input, there is often modification of the interactional structure of conversations involving NNSs. For example, there may be more interruptions from the main line of conversation than in conversations with NSs. This is referred to as *modified interaction*.

Native Languages: Mixed
Target Language: English
Background Information: Adults
Data Source: Conversations

Data

Native speakers in conversations with nonnative speakers.

1. Did you *like* San Diego?
2. Did you *like* San Diego? San Diego did you like it?
3. Right. When do you take the break? At ten-thirty?
4. *NS:* When do you go to the uh Santa Monica? You say you go fishing in Santa Monica, right?
   NNS: Yeah
   NS: When?
5. *NS:* Uh what does uh what does your father do in uh you're from Kyoto, right?
   NNS: yeah
   NS: What does your father do in Kyoto?
6. *NS:* Are you going to visit San Francisco? or Las Vegas?
   NNS: Yes I went to Disneyland and to Knottsberry Farm
   NS: oh yeah?
7. *NS:* Do you like California?
   NNS: Huh?
   NS: Do you like Los Angeles?
   NNS: uhm
   NS: Do you like California?
   NNS: Oh! yeah I like

Questions

1. Describe the ways in which these native speakers ask nonnative speakers questions.

2. What do you think the communicative effect is of asking questions in this way?

PROBLEM 6.2

Native Languages: Mixed
Target Language: English
Background Information: Adult ESL students, beginning and advanced
Data Source: Responses to questions by NNSs asking for directions to the train station.

Part I

Data

1. *Q:* Please I need information about the station train. (NNS)
   A: Train station? I can tell you where it is. (NS)
2. *Q:* Can you tell me where the train station is? (NS)

   A: Train station . . . (NS)
3. *Q:* I need information about the train station . . . Do you know? (NNS)
   A: . . . where [the] train station is. Yes . . . (NS)
4. *Q:* Can you tell me how to get to the train station from here? (NS)
   A: Oh, sure. Go up . . . (NS)

Questions

1. How would you categorize these four types of responses?

2. What is the difference between them?

3. Consider the differences between the responses to NNSs as opposed to NSs. What function can you suggest for the different response types?

Part II

Data

Number of responses for each of the four categories as per Part I.

	Low-Level ESL	*Upper-Level ESL*	*Native Speakers*
1.	12	12	1
2.	2	4	6
3.	4	—	—
4.	6	8	17

Questions

4. Based on these figures, does your answer to question 2 change? In what ways are responses to nonnatives different from responses to native speakers?

5. In what ways are the responses to the more advanced level nonnatives different from those to low-level nonnatives?

6. In what ways are the responses to advanced ESL speakers similar to those of native speakers?

*7. How do these responses fit in with traditional notions of foreigner talk?

*8. Redefine the concept of foreigner talk to include data such as those presented in this problem.

PROBLEM 6.3

Native Language: Spanish
Target Language: English
Background Information: Adult ESL students
Data Source: Discussion of three stories, all of which include ranking in terms of which character (1) is the most reprehensible, (2) should be saved, and (3) is the most useful for survival at sea

Part I

Data

Below are ways in which native speakers and nonnative speakers express agreement.

Native speakers
Immediate

1. That's the same as mine.
2. Well, that's close.
3. We're kind of agreed on some of them.
4. Well, I thought she was pretty bad too, but . . .

After some discussion

5. I could go along with switching a little bit.
6. Well, I'm somewhat convinced by what you say.
7. That is somewhat good idea, I guess, in the extreme case.
8. I think basically you have a somewhat legitimate argument.

Nonnative speakers
Immediate

1. Well, in the first, third we have the same.
2. It's agree, no? We're agree.
3. We are agree.

After some discussion

4. All right.
5. I changed my mind.
6. I am agree. I can change it.
7. It's OK. I think is OK.
8. Yeah, I change to seven.

Questions

1. How do the native speakers express agreement?

2. How do the nonnative speakers express agreement?

3. What similarities/differences are there between NSs and NNSs in expressing agreement?

Data

Below are ways in which native speakers and nonnative speakers express disagreement.

Native speakers

1. (I ranked them—those two the worst.) Really. I ranked Abigail and Slug the worst.
2. At this point, I was very arbitrary.
3. But I don't know how it works.
4. I thought . . . but who would know for sure.
5. Oh! It didn't even enter my head.
6. I wouldn't necessarily agree with that.
7. So I had him kind of towards the end of my list.

Nonnative speakers

1. No!
2. Well, I disagree with you.
3. I'm no agree with that.
4. But that is not important.
5. Is wrong.
6. No, no, forget it!
7. I'm not sure about
8. Is very difficult
9. I didn't really pay attention of that part.

Questions

4. How do the NSs express disagreement?

5. How do the NNSs express disagreement?

6. What similarities/differences are there between NSs and NNSs in expressing disagreement?

*7. How are agreement and disagreement expressed differently by (a) NSs and (b) NNSs?

PROBLEM 6.4

Native Languages: Mixed
Target Language: English
Background Information: Adults with varying amounts of proficiency
Data Source: Free conversation and picture description

Data

1. *NS:* We have five people, I'm the only girl, I'm the oldest
   NNS: oh, you're the oldest
   NS: and two—I have two younger brothers
   NNS: I see, so the other two will be sisters?
   NS: no
   NNS: oh, including your parents, oh I see
   NS: only three kids
2. *NNS:* Did somebody give you money-uh-put in the red bug
   NS: red packet
   NNS: yeah red packet
3. *NNS:* and four angle is same
   NS: four angles
   NNS: angles are same
4. *NS:* Do you think he may come to Hawaii?
   NNS: um-I think-uh-maybe he graduate-uh-he finish school
   NS: when he finishes
   NNS: yeah
   NS: and then come
   NNS: yes he come, when he finishes, he come

Questions

1. Focus on the corrections made by the NSs. What type of information is being corrected in each case?

2. What differences are there in the way the NS makes corrections?

3. What kind of generalization(s) can you make about the way different kinds of correcting devices are used, based on the information which is being corrected?

4. Based on these data, do the corrections seem to work? In what way?

*5. What is the difficulty in claiming that the corrections "work" given data of this sort?

PROBLEM 6.5

Native Language: Spanish
Target Language: English
Background Information: Adult university students, living in the United States since before age 7
Data Source: Informal conversations

Part I

Data

1. *Context:* J and P are talking about sports. (J is an English L1 speaker. P is a native Spanish speaker. Both are males.)

   J: Do you golf?
   P: No I . . .
   J: No. Neither do I. uhm What are you majoring in?

2. *Context:* A and L (both male, native speakers of English)

   A: And what's your maj ⌐ or?

   L: ⌐ I'm a cinema television major.
   A: And what do you do when you graduate with that?
   L: I hope to be a director one day.
   A: Real ⌐ ly?

   L: ⌐ A real live director.
   A: Of television or movie?
   L: Television
   A: Television
   L: Why television opposed to movies?
   A: 'Cuz television is what everything's switching to because of cable tv. So it interests me.

Questions

1. Consider the linking of topics, that is, the way in which topics are connected throughout the conversation. Are there differences between the NS/NNS interaction and the NS/NS interaction? If so, how are they different?

Part II

Data

3. *Context:* P and J discover that P used to live in the same dormitory as J. (P is the native Spanish speaker and J is the L1 speaker. Both are males.)

   P: They have a very good school here ⌐ from what I know.

   J: ⌐ Yeah they do.
   P: Yeah they do.
   J: Yeah
   P: So where do you live?
   J: uhm On campus
   P: uhum
   J: I live in Residence West.
   P: Oh really? What floor?
   J: I'm on eight.

P: Oh real⌐ly
J: └ Do you live there?
P: I used to live there last ⌐year.
J: └ Oh really? So did I.

... conversation proceeds with no abrupt topic shifts for 25 seconds.

J: Oh you are I was in 80- I mean I was in 1003 (ten-0-three) in the uh D room. (giggle)
P: Isn't that weird? Oh my God. Where are you living now?

Questions

2. Again consider the concept of linking. Does this conversation between a NS and an NNS show evidence of linking? In this regard is it more similar to conversation 1 or 2 of Part I?

3. Account for any similarities that you see between the conversation in 3 and the one that is most similar to it (1 or 2).

PROBLEM 6.6

Native Languages: Japanese and Spanish
Target Language: English
Background Information: Adults, ranging in proficiency from beginners to high intermediate, enrolled in an ESL program
Data Source: Informal conversations: J = Japanese L1, S = Spanish L1

=== Part I ===

Data

1. *S:* When are you going to visit me?
   J: Pardon me?
2. *S:* When can you go to visit me?
   J: visit?
3. *J:* . . . research
   J: Research, I don't know the meaning.
4. *S:* What is your name?
   S: My name?
   S: yeah
5. *S:* But he work with uh uh institution
   J: institution
   S: Do you know that?
6. *J:* Are you a student in your country?
   S: in my class?
   J: in your country?
   S: Oh, I don't understand.
   J: OK OK so what did you do in your country?
7. *S:* What is your purpose for studying English in Ann Arbor?
   S: (silence)
   S: What is your purpose for studying English?
8. *J:* yeah. How long . . . will you be? will you be staying?
   J: I will 4 months
   J: 4 months?
   J: stay 4 months here until April
9. *S:* . . . and and the condition for uh bets my level in my company it necessary my speaking English
   S: hm you mean that English is important in your company to (indiscernible)

Questions

1. Concentrate on the indications of nonunderstanding. What devices do these NNSs use to indicate that they have not fully comprehended the previous utterance?

Data

1. Average number of indications of nonunderstanding in 5 minutes of transcribed data

Type of interaction	Indications of nonunderstanding
NS-NS	0.50
NS-NNS	2.75
NNS-NNS	10.29

2. Average number of indications of nonunderstanding in 5 minutes of transcribed data from NNS-NNS dyads

Group 1 Same language, same proficiency	Group 2 Same language, different proficiency	Group 3 Different language, same proficiency	Group 4 Different language, different proficiency
4 dyads	3 dyads	4 dyads	3 dyads
$\bar{x} = 4.75$	$\bar{x} = 10.67$	$\bar{x} = 11.25$	$\bar{x} = 16.00$
s.d. $= 0.50$	s.d. $= 3.79$	s.d. $= 2.99$	s.d. $= 3.00$

Questions

2. Consider 1 in Part II. How would you account for the differences found among the three different kinds of conversational dyads?

3. Consider 2 in Part II. What explanation can you give for the differences among the four groups of NNSs?

*4. Can you give a single explanation to account for the data in 1 and 2 of Part II?

Native Languages: Mixed
Target Language: English
Background Information: Adult ESL learners
Data Source: Native speaker ratings of NNS' readings of sentences

Data

Below are 28 sentences read by NNSs on which 27 NSs of English gave pronunciation ratings (good or bad TL pronunciation).

| | Number of responses | | |
Sentence	Good	Bad	Read by subject no.
1. He is unusual to have a new car.	8	19	1
2. He does spend his holidays always at home.	2	25	2
3. We had to water the garden because it didn't rain yesterday.	0	27	3
4. My nephew grew up while he was in college.	15	12	4
5. It is necessary for finish the work.	14	13	5
6. He said that he has no money.	25	1	6
7. He writes not good books.	4	23	7
8. I am sorry that he was disappointed.	27	0	8
9. An active president has chosen our country.	7	20	9
10. His behavior will lead him to prison.	3	24	10
11. They are interested in horses riding.	19	8	11
12. He always spends his holidays at home.	10	17	2
13. He doesn't write good books.	22	5	7
14. I prevented him to going with me.	2	25	12
15. They are interested in riding horses.	19	8	11
16. Nowhere do you can see so many people.	26	1	13
17. I prevented him from going with me.	14	13	12
18. Our country has chosen an active president.	17	10	9
19. Nowhere can you see so many people.	26	1	13
20. It is unusual for him to have a new car.	26	1	1
21. He said that he no money has.	3	24	6
22. My nephew was grown up while he was in college.	17	10	4
23. I am waiting until find rich man.	4	17	14
24. His behavior will lead to go to prison.	6	21	10
25. I am sorry for him be disappointed.	16	11	8
26. It is necessary in order to finish the work.	25	2	5
27. I am waiting until I find a rich man.	24	3	14
28. We had to water the garden after it hadn't rained yesterday.	0	27	3

Questions

1. Consider the sentences read by each individual subject. Describe the relationship between these sentences.

2. Given the above data, what factor(s) do you think entered into decisions about the quality of NNS pronunciation?

══════ **Part II** ══════

Data

Below are transcriptions by a NS of English of the sentences given in Part I. (The subject heard each sentence only once.)

1. It is unusual for have a new car.
2. He does spend . . . . at home.
3. We had . . . . because it didn't rain yesterday.
4. My nephew grew up when he was in college.
5. It is necessary for finish the work.
6. He said that he has no money.
7. He likes not good books.
8. I'm sorry that he was disappointed.
9. An ectic president has chosen our country.
10. . . . .
11. They are interested in horses riding.
12. Hold his pants . . . . his . . . . at home.
13. He doesn't write good books.
14. I permitted him to going with me.
15. But am interested in riding horses.
16. Nowhere do you can see so many people.
17. I prevented him from going with me.
18. Our country has chosen an active president.
19. Nowhere can you see so many people.
20. It is unusual for him to have a new car.
21. He said that he not manage this.
22. My nephew was grown up while he was in college.
23. I am waiting on the fine ridge now.
24. His girlfriend will leave to go to visit.
25. I am sorry for him to be disappointed.
26. It is necessary in order to finish the work.
27. I am waiting until I find a rich man.
28. We had to water the garden after it rained yesterday.

Questions

3. Based on this transcription, how would you determine which of these sentences was the easiest to understand?

4. What objective criteria did you use in question 3 to determine comprehensibility of NNS speech?

5. Order the sentences from most easy to understand to least easy.

6. Based on your results of the previous questions, can you make a generalization about which sentences are easiest to understand and why?

*7. Considering the results of Parts I and II, what factor(s) are involved in understanding NNS speech?

**8. In what way is comprehensibility a function of interacting factors?

Native Languages: Japanese, Arabic, Urdu, and Korean
Target Language: English
Background Information: Kindergarten children
Data Source: Spontaneous utterances

══════ Part I ══════

Data

1.   Teacher instructions to a kindergarten class of primarily NSs:
     These are babysitters taking care of babies.
     Draw a line from Q to q. From S to s and then trace.
2.   Same teacher giving instructions to a single NS:
     Now, Johnny, you have to make a great big pointed hat.
3.   Same teacher to mid-level Urdu speaker:
     Now her hat is big. Pointed.
4.   Same teacher to low-medium-level Arabic speaker:
     See hat? Hat is big. Big and tall.
5.   Same teacher to low-level Japanese speaker (1) and low-level Korean speaker (2):
     1. Big, big, big hat.
     2. baby sitter.   baby.

Questions

1. How do the five types of teacher speech differ?

2. What do these data suggest about the ways teachers talk to students of varying proficiency levels?

══════ Part II ══════

Data

A.

Student	Proficiency level	% teacher utterances[1]	Teacher MLU[2]	NL
1	Low	40.5	3.18	Japanese
2	Low-medium	27.9	3.37	Arabic
3	Medium	14.9	4.51	Urdu
4	Native speaker	16.0	5.27	English

[1]Total teacher utterances = 269
[2]MLU = mean length of utterance

B.

	Word Usage	
Student	% total items[3]	Type/Token
1	37.62	0.33
2	24.75	0.41
3	14.50	0.59
4	23.47	0.48

Questions

3. Do the data in A strengthen or disconfirm the conclusions you drew in Part I?

4. What additional information do the data in B provide?

*5. What uniform explanation can you give to account for the data presented in Parts I and II?

[3]Total vocabulary items = 933

SECTION 7

Specific-Purpose Acquisition

In this section, the following concepts should prove useful:

1. Specific purpose
2. Rhetoric

Specific purpose refers to goal-oriented language in a well-delineated setting, e.g., English for Medical Purposes, French for Business Purposes.

Rhetoric here refers to the organizational choices that a speaker or writer makes in his/her discourse, e.g., whether to define or classify something, whether to be general or to provide specific details.

Native Language: Spanish
Target Language: English
Background Information: Second semester MA student in civil engineering in the United States
Data Source: Video-taped interview and playback sessions

Data

S is an English for Academic Purposes specialist who is trying to get L, the civil engineering student, to explain the technical term *acceleration* as it relates to costs and the scheduling of construction projects. *Claims* in this context is a technical term in the legal sense. In the transcript, the vertical lines indicate overlaps and the numbers in parentheses indicate pauses in seconds.

S: Can you explain to me what acceleration means?

L: I understood for acceleration when you want to get the project eh—faster than the normal eschedule for example if you eh have one year (2) you want to get the project done eh ten months you have to accelerate the project to (1) maybe to use eh overtime I mean (1) (in the equal) instead of work eight hours a day you can work eh ten hours or twelve hours (1) to (1) get (1) time

S: so it means to make the ah project go faster

L: faster—exactly

S: and there's a lot of ss- ah claims about acceleration—is that the point (2) or no

L: (was) I think that it's no (4) acceleration in this case you can see the owner the architect and the engineers | | are in the | defensive

S: | Right | | the defense

L: positions |

S: | uh huh

L: and the contractor, subcontractors I mean the people who make the (laugh) the project are in the other position—offensive | | position—

| now wh—|

S: —why is that do you think

L: I think that the (3) I—how can I (4) I think that in acceleration in this case is more expensive for the contractor and for the subcontractor make the project faster (2) (I) mean you ah first you have to show to the owner why is more expensive (1) because you want to make the project more faster (1) you have to pay eh more (1) more labor more materials and but you have to show that (1) and usually you have to go to arbitration to (1) or in this case claims (2) you have to show to the owner why you espent more money doing faster the project (2) and the owner doesn't want to pay | | because he feels usually he feels that ah is the:e time

S: | Right |

L: you spend twelve months or ten months doing one project he feels that ah cost of the project is the same and thats not true?

S: It depends on—

L: You want to get the project eh done faster you have to use eh overtime you have to pay more labor (1) instead of use for example ten laborers (1) you have to use fifteen or twenty (1) and you have to pay more labor (3) there is a (3) something I think is something about costs

S: costs

L: (in) the project ...

Questions

1. Describe how this learner, as the expert in the technical field, uses repetition in the information he gives to the interviewer. Specify your criteria for what constitutes repetition.

2. How does this learner use *exactly*? What effect is achieved by *exactly* and the disagreement structure that follows?

3. How are generalizations and specific details used by the learner in his attempt to explain *acceleration* to the interviewer?

4. What are the various uses of *you* in this conversation, and how are they related to the learner's attempt to explain *acceleration* to the interviewer?

*5. Sum up the rhetoric (general/specific, repetition, disagreement, etc.) and the flow of information in this conversation.

PROBLEM 7.2

Native Language: Spanish
Target Language: English
Background Information: Second semester MA student in civil engineering in the United States
Data Source: Video-taped interview and playback sessions

Data

Below are presented episodes from two conversations, with the same nonnative speaker in both. In the first, S, an English for Academic Purposes specialist, is trying to get L, the civil engineering student, to explain the term *critical path schedules* from a technical article that both had read. The second conversation involves two former friends, who had not seen each other for six months, chatting on general topics. In the first conversation, both participants are male, in the second P is a female. In the transcript, the vertical lines indicate overlaps and the numbers in parentheses indicate pauses in seconds.

1. *S:* "... both the contractor and the owner maintained critical path schedules on the project." What's a critical path?

   L: Critical path, for example—the critical path is the more important activities you have to do in doing the project. Let's say for example you have fi' activities (1) OK? (3) you have fi' activities (1) and in order to make this activity you have to wait until this activity is make—is make (2) this is three—this is three | four

   S: | You can't put the — you can't put the floor in until you put the columns

   L: | Exactly

   S: | Something like that?

   L: OK and say this is the floor ah this is the columns and this is the the roof

   S: Right

   L: OK? goes goes in this way but when you're doing this you can make you put the the the floor already or the fundations sss—let's say that this is foundations, columns and roof

   S: OK

   L: You can—you should—you must wait until you have made the foundations to start with the columns

   S: Right

   L: and you have to wait un- until you can make the columns to start with the roof? because the columns will support the roof?

....

2. *L:* ... but it is only in in Mexico you can find that meat in Sonora. I don't know is the only place who (1) which (3) it used to do that with the with the meat

   P: I think I had that before—do you make it into ah tacos? | because its

   L: | Like in burritos?

   P: um hmmm

   L: OK

   P: It's (like eating) burritos | | in in your part not tacos

   L: | Yes | No it's tacos—but with that kind of meat you you you do burritos

   P: Um hmm ...

Questions

1. In the technical episode, describe the strategy(ies) the learner uses in attempting to explain the civil engineering concept *critical path schedules.*

2. In the technical episode, the interviewer, S, in his second turn tries to help move the conversation along by suggesting an exemplary construction model. In doing so, he uses the wrong technical term (*floor*) from the point of view of the learner/expert. Describe the correction strategy(ies) used by the learner as the "expert/knower" in the technical field. How does the learner, as the expert/knower in the technical field, correct the interviewer?

3. In the playback session, when the learner/expert was asked why he had corrected the interviewer at this point, he stated:

   > Because is—in structural—in structures you have the the support of the columns is—are the— the foundation—the floor is—is not supporting anything but I didn't explain him . . . I think that in that part I did good because I am studying that—I'm taking a course of that—I think that he understood that—that part because he said "I see I see."

   Describe how this information shows the learner, as technical expert, confirming his professional stance.

4. In the matching nontechnical episode, L, the NNS, is talking with a different interviewer about more casual matters. He is describing the northern Mexican dish, machaca, and the preparation of the meat that goes into it. How does he go about presenting this information?

5. As in the technical episode, we here see the interviewer making an error, in this case confusing tacos with burritos. What correction strategy(ies) are used here by L?

*6. Compare the modes of correction used by L in the two episodes, the technical and nontechnical. Consider in your answer such concepts as politeness, mitigation, and precision of language.

Native Language: Spanish
Target Language: English
Background Information: Second semester MA student in civil engineering in the United States
Data Source: Video-taped interview and playback sessions

Data

Below are presented episodes from two conversations with the same nonnative speaker in both. In the first, L, a civil engineering student, is trying to explain to S, an English for Academic Purposes expert, about the various factors that are involved in the breakdown of construction equipment. The second conversation involves two former friends, who have not seen each other for six months, chatting on general topics. In the first conversation, both participants are male, in the second, P is a female. In the transcript, the vertical lines indicate overlaps and the numbers in parentheses indicate pauses in seconds. Finally, "Farmer Jack" is the name of a supermarket.

1. *L:* ... and then this is eff (2) eh (3) referring that the contractor maybe didn't adjust the equipment to the co—site conditions maybe this you know the equipment can be effected by the the (3) what is that the (3) I lost the word (1) I mean (2) because no (1) for—you have one equipment here in for example in one estate (1) and you want to move that equipment to for example you are working Michigan and you want to move that equipment to Arizona or a higher estate (2) you have to adjust your equipment because the productivity of the equipment eh gets down (1) eh because of the different eh height of the | (project) | place

   S: | Oh I see | the a the ah altitude

   L: Yeah the altitude—that | is the word

   S: | that's the word

   L: I was looking for

   S: Yeah the altitude—the altitude makes a difference

   L: makes a difference in the productivity of the equipment.

   . . . .

2. *L:* ... sent to us ah (2) Mexican food like ah tortillas - like ah | (2) machaca

   P: | oooh

   L: I don't know if you know what is—what machaca is

   P: Tell me—I think I've had it once before

   L: No—you you get some meat and you put that meat eh to the sun

   P: Um hmmm

   L: til the meat like eh to cook that meat but only with the sun an after that you (2) I don't know what is (3) I—I learned that name because when I went to the (1) 'sss—Farmer Jack I saw that—you make like a little a thin (3) oh my god (3) then you—you (2) forget it (laugh)

   P: (laugh) make it into strips?

   L: OK like a—you you have a steak no? | | you first you put that esteak

   P: | uh huh |

   L: In the sun—you have

   P: then it gets rotten and you throw it away

   L: ummm—no no no no no only one day or two days

   P: Um hmmm

   L: after that with a stone (2) you like escramble that (1) like ah—

   P: You grind it up?

   L: Yes that psss you you start to (3) what is that word (1) oh my god—

   P: Mash?

L:	Exactly—you have to you start making mash			that meat (2)
P:			um hmmm	
L:	and after that they you can eat it eat that meat and it's very very. . . .

Questions

1. In the technical episode, describe the learner/expert's communication strategy(ies) as he attempts to deal with a missing vocabulary item. Describe the interaction when the learner finally accesses a synonym, *height*.

2. In the matching, nontechnical episode, the NNS, L, is talking about food and, as in the technical episode, he also attempts to deal with a missing vocabulary item. Describe his communication strategy(ies) as he attempts to deal with this missing item.

*3. Compare the communication strategy(ies) used in dealing with missing vocabulary items in the two episodes, technical and nontechnical. Compare the interaction when the learner accesses a synonym here, too (*escramble*).

*4. Compare the learner's use of *exactly* here with his use of the word in the data in Problem 7.1.

**5. In the nontechnical episodes of both problems 7.2 and 7.3, L is talking to a female about food and its preparation, whereas in the technical episodes (as well as in the data of Problem 7.1), L is talking to S, a male. How does this information affect your answers to the questions in these three problems?

**6. A playback session with a different informant (a linguist specializing in discourse analysis)—while viewing the video tapes underlying the transcripts in problems 7.1, 7.2, and 7.3—yielded the following: In the technical episodes, L does not resort to the use of gestures but instead relies almost exclusively on verbal strategies to get his meaning across. In the nontechnical episodes, in contrast, his performance is full of expression, gesture, and movement. How does this information, along with the information in question 4, affect your answers to the questions in these problems?

PROBLEM 7.4

Native Language: Mandarin
Target Language: English
Background Information: MA student in computer engineering in the United States
Data Source: Compositions from a pre- "English for Academic Purposes" course in an intensive program

=== **Part I** ===

Data

Safe Rules: Students in this composition course were given examples of rhetorical "safe rules," i.e., pedagogical statements about the organization of writing which if followed by the student *should* allow the writing to be understood as intended. Two of the safe rules these students were asked to follow in writing their compositions are:

Safe Rule 1: Topic statement: To begin a paragraph safely, write a statement that has two parts: (a) a main, controlling or "core idea" which is the topic of the entire paragraph; (b) a hint of development of the paragraph, e.g., chronological, spatial, contrast.

Safe Rule 2: Comparison and contrast: In comparing or contrasting any X or Y, there are two safe choices (a) and (b): (a) Compare X and Y point by point in "pairs": x_1, y_1; x_2, y_2; x_3, y_3, etc. (b) Compare X and Y in "blocks" with all of the comparative details written for X first and then for Y: $x_{1,2,3,...}$; $y_{1,2,3,...}$; etc. Also (c) Do not mix (a) and (b); that is not safe. And (d) Be sure to use *explicit* contrastive connectives, e.g., *yet, however, on the other hand.*

Compositions: The following composition was written in response to the directive: "Describe something that is significant to you about the USA, relating that to something in your country."

Original:

The College Students in China look so different from those in U.S.A. in many ways; the way they study; the way they live; and the way they think. American Students always study individually, their Chinese counterparts off after work in groups, discussing problems together. While American Students are enjoying their parties on Friday night. Known as party night, Chinese students probably are studying at the libraries for their exam the next day. If Americans view their study at college as the investment for the future, Chinese Students value it as exit to higher social status since in China only 2 to 3 per cent of the high school graduates can get into colleges.

Rewrite 1 (after professor/student consultation):

College students in China look so different from those in U.S.A. in many ways: the way they study, the way they live, and even the way they think. Showing their famous personalities in college life, American students always study individually. Instead their Chinese counterparts often work in groups, discussing problems together. While American students are enjoying their parties on Friday night, known as party night, Chinese students probably are studying at libraries for their next day's exam because in China workweek is from Monday to Saturday. If Americans view their studies at college as an investment for the future because they pay for the education, Chinese students value it as an exit to higher social status since only two to three per cent of high school graduates can get into colleges.

In short, the differences between college students in these two countries are rooted in the base of the cultural difference. They are only some examples of it.

Questions

1. Describe the rhetorical or organizational choices made by the learner in the original composition in terms of Safe Rule 1.

2. Describe the rhetorical or organizational choices made by the learner in the original composition in terms of Safe Rule 2.

3. Describe the changes, if any, from the original to rewrite 1 in terms of Safe Rules 1 and 2.

===== **Part II** =====

Data

Compositions: The following compositions were written by the same learner one week later in response to the directive: "Compare and contrast the advantages and disadvantages of advertising."

Original:

    We can view advertisement in both positive and negative ways. From the point of economics, advertisement is essential to most business activities. Good advertisements could impress consumers so much that they might give prior consideration to a certain products. In addition, advertisement could produce a good "public image" for producer. Once such a "image" is established a business organization can improve and develop its relation with other business organizations with little difficulties. One can say that advertisement is a kind of skills for business survival and development. Advertisement has its negative aspects. As a matter of fact. Many producers exaggerate the function of their products in their advertisements. They may mislead the consumers. On the other hand, some advertisements involve the problems of morality. They are claimed so often the spiritual health of people, especially young people.

Rewrite 1 (after professor/student consultation):

    We can view advertisement in two ways: both positive and negative. From the point of economics, advertisement is essential to most business activities. Good advertisement could impress consumers so much that they might give a prior consideration to a certain product. In addition, advertisement could produce a good "image" for a producer. once such an "image" is established, a business organization can improve and develop its relation with others with little difficulties. One can say that advertisement is a kind of skills for business survival and development.

    Advertisement, however, has its negative aspects. As a matter of fact, many producers often exaggerate the functions of their products in their advertisements. Moreover, involve the problem of morality. Such advertisements are claimed to affect the spiritual health of people, especially young people.

Questions

4. Describe the rhetorical or organizational choices made by the learner in the original composition in terms of Safe Rule 1.

5. Describe the rhetorical or organizational choices made by the learner in the original composition in terms of Safe Rule 2.

6. Describe the changes, if any, from the original to rewrite 1 in terms of Safe Rules 1 and 2.

*7. Look at Parts I and II in a chronological sense. Describe rhetorical changes and nonchanges over time in terms of Safe Rules 1 and 2. Relate any changes you discover to the concept "acquisition" and any nonchanges to the concept "possible rhetorical fossilization."

===== Part III =====

Data

Composition: The following composition was written by the same learner three weeks later in response to the directive: "Take two important concepts in your subject matter and contrast them."

Original:

In a computer, bit is the most basic block. Each bit's state represents either "0" or "1" Address, however, a location of data. Address is specified by characters. Each character occupies a certain number of bits (For IBM 360/370, a character consists of 8 bits). Conceptually speaking, bits are found in all parts of central processing unit (CPU) yet addresses are only the components of the storage. Which is part of CPU. While bits can form any instruction command.

Rewrite: There was no time in the 8-week course for a rewrite.

Questions

8. Describe the rhetorical or organizational choices made by the learner in this composition in terms of Safe Rule 1.

9. Describe the rhetorical or organizational choices made by the learner in this composition in terms of Safe Rule 2.

*10. Sum up the three compositions in terms of (1) changes and nonchanges over time and (2) Safe Rules 1 and 2 (and other possible safe rules, e.g., definition, classification), relating any changes you discover to acquisition and any nonchanges to possible rhetorical fossilization.

PROBLEM 7.5

Native Languages: German (TA1) and Spanish (TA2)
Target Language: English
Background Information: Two math teaching assistants (TA) in a university class: TA1: considered to be a "good" TA; TA2: considered to "have problems" as a TA
Data Source: Video-tapes of classes

Part I

Data

TA1: At the beginning of the class session, the TA asked if there were any questions. A student asked a question about a homework problem. He first read the problem silently to himself and then responded: Ok what's what's the variable we can change? Uh, well... we wanna minimize the inventory costs, right? And what does that depend on? What's the decision we wanna make?

TA2: Beginning of the class session: I want to finish section 4.4 ... and some problems and ... then ... I'll do most of section 4.5 we can have 2 sessions for review ... eh ... section 4.4 ... there are some other problems, on the Mean Value Theorem, Rolle's Theorem ... and ... uh ... well there is one more problem, ... a couple of problems I want to try in this section ... number 21 ... we have a ball ... that is thrown upwards for a window here we have a window, so building (draws)

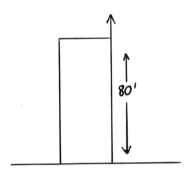

and the ball is thrown up ... the window is 80 feet above the ground level ... and ... uh ... velocity ... initial velocity of the ball

Questions

1. What differences do you notice in the way the TAs introduce the class? How do they differ in the way they introduce a specific problem?

2. Describe how different viewpoints in terms of audience awareness are reflected in these data.

Part II

Data

TA1: The class has arrived at the equation

$$\text{Total cost } C(x) = 0.9 \cdot \frac{600}{2x} + x \cdot 30$$

... OK now we're gonna minimize this one ... so what do I do?

S: take the derivative

T: yeah, OK now we're at the easy part again ... and the derivative of the first summand is what? ... Well the 0.9 times 600 over 2 ... What's the derivative of $1/x$?

S: $-1/x^2$

T: -1 over x^2, good. What's the derivative of $30x$?

S: 30

T: OK we wanna solve this for zero

$$C'(x) = \frac{0.9\,(600)}{2}\left(\frac{-1}{x^2}\right) + 30$$

$$= 0$$

that means

$$30 = \frac{-0.9 \times 600}{2} \cdot \frac{1}{x^2}$$

S: is that right?

S: no, the 30 should be negative

T: yeah it better be otherwise there would certainly not be good OK or

$$x^2 = 0.9\,\frac{600}{60}$$

which is 0.9 times 10

$$= 9$$

so

$$x = \pm 3$$

and of course I couldn't care less about -3. ... OK is this a maximum or minimum?

S: minimum

T: what's the best thing to do now? ... well

S: sign diagram?

T: I think the second derivative is easier. See if you take the second derivative then this factor drops out and you just have $C''(x)$ equals this constant factor 0.9(600)/2 and only thing you care about is that it's positive ... times then you have the -1 here. ... what's the derivative of $1/x^2$?

S: 2/2 no

S: (.....)

T: see think about this as x^{-2}

S: 2

T: it's minus $2x$ to the -3

S: (.....) $-2x^{-3}$

T: right see it's $-2x^{-3}$ and if you forget the minus then you screw everything up because you have just missed the sign of this and you make terrible mistakes, so x^{-2} you pull the -2 across and you get the exponent (.....) so this thing is positive

$$C''(x) = \frac{0.9\,(600)}{2}\,(-1)\,(-2)\,x^{-3}$$

$$> 0$$

and if you plug in 3, a positive value, then the entire thing is positive

$$C''(3) > 0$$

so what do I get?

S: minimum

T: minimum, which is what I wanted

$$C''(3) > 0 \rightarrow \min$$

TA2: The class has arrived at the equation

$$s(t) = -16t^2 + 64t + 80$$

now the highest point is reached when you ... eh ... what what is the condition for the highest point? you can find, in an ... any of these equations, I mean look for it, look for a condition which set one of these equations the one for acceleration one for velocity or the one for ... position. ... What happens when the ball reaches the highest point?

S: velocity is 0

T: the velocity is zero it is stopped momentarily at that point now you can tell that just by physical considerations the ball has to get to a full stop before it starts going downward ... so that's just for a physical consideration but ... by a mathematical consideration you know that the that s is a maximum when the first derivative is zero ... first derivative of s is velocity so that's the condition we want

$$v = 0$$

ok ... when is v equal 0? ok ... we come up with the equation

$$-32t + 64 = 0$$

therefore t equal 64 over 32

$$t = \frac{64}{32} = 2$$

2 seconds ... at that time the ball reaches the highest point in its trajectory and we have a question here ... how high does it go? how can we find the point ... we know the time ... we want the position ... so must ... see ... use the equation for s, so

$$s(2) = -16(4) + 64(2) + 80$$

and that is

$$= -64 + 128 + 80$$
$$= 144 \text{ feet}$$

Questions

3. What strategies do these TAs use to "talk through" the solutions? To answer this you will have to separate out (a) the math from (b) the talk about the math. You might want to focus on turn changes within the two conversations.

4. Does one TA ask more questions that the other? Do the types of questions differ? If so, how?

5. Do the TAs attempt to paraphrase? If so, in what contexts?

==== **Part III** ====

Data

TA1: The class has arrived at the answer (in Part II). See it's useful to develop an eye when the sign diagram is faster and when the second derivative is faster. Usually in a case like this we just have a sum of powers of x, and $1/x$ is a power of x, then it's much faster to compute the second derivative. On the other hand if you have a quotient, where the quotient rule gets you in a big mess or say you have to use the chain rule and that's complicated, then it might be faster to use a sign diagram. If you have the thing already factored, then the sign diagram is usually fast, and the second derivative is usually slow, so it might save you five valuable minutes if you're able to use the right procedure. OK so that was a hard example something like that is not going to be on the test.

TA2: The group has arrived at the answer:

$$= -96$$

. . . negative velocity means that the ball is going in the . . . negative direction of the axis when the particle is moving in the positive direction you have positive velocity when it is negative direction you have negative velocities, so that's that problem and eh that's called . . . this section is . . . in 27 you have eh you have

Questions

6. How do each of the TAs close the topic?

*7. Looking at the data from Parts I, II, and III, what comparison can you make between the two TAs relating to their use of questions and responses, change of topics, and structure of explanations?

PROBLEM 7.6

Native Language: Tagalog
Target Language: English
Background Information: Two Filipino nurses on trial. They were convicted of conspiracy and of poisoning patients. A new trial was ordered, and later the charges were dropped.
Data Source: Transcripts of a legal trial

===== Part I =====

Data

Q. Would you say that the two of you were close friends during that period of time?
A. I would say we are good friends but we are really not that close because I don't know her and we don't know each other that much.

Additional information: Earlier during the course of the trial, the defendant had testified that she had become good friends with the person being discussed.

Information about Tagalog tense/aspect system: Tense is not marked on the verb. Thus, **eats/is eating/was eating** is all expressed by the same verb form. **ate/has eaten/had eaten** are expressed by a single verb form.

Questions

1. How does the example above appear to contradict her earlier statement concerning her relationship with another person?

2. What appears to be the basis of the confusion?

===== Part II =====

Data

Q. Weren't you a relief supervisor for about six, seven months?
A. I think I started in December of '74.
Q. '74 until about June of '75?
A. Yes.
Q. So, are you saying that some time during that time you learned about Pavulon?
A. Yes.
Q. And what else did you learn about Pavulon, other than it was given at surgery?
→ A. Are you asking me about what I know about Pavulon in the summer of '75 or what I know about Pavulon at the present time, after hearing all these experts?
Q. What you knew about Pavulon at the time.
A. I know a little about Pavulon.
Q. What did you know about it?
A. I know it's used in anesthesia.

149

Q. Why? Or, what else do you know about it?

A. When I work in ICU, I learn that it's used to a patient to relax. It's a muscle relaxant. The patient should be on a respirator and it should be ordered by a doctor.

Questions

3. Does the misunderstanding (indicated by the arrow) in this conversation have the same source as the one in Part I? Why? or why not?

======= **Part III** =======

Data

1. *Q.* How did you feel when you arrived here in the United States?

   A. When I was in the airplane? When I arrive, I was very homesick because that is the first time I would be away from my parents. . . .

2. *Q.* How did you feel when you came to the Veterans Hospital and found out that the understaffing was worse?

   A. I didn't know that until I was in the V.A.

3. *Q.* Well, you did say that you looked at the chart.

   A. I looked at the chart when? When do you want?

   Q. I don't know when. You said you looked at the chart. Did you not say that you looked at the chart?

   A. I'd been saying I looked at the charts many times since we started this investigation.

4. *Q.* It is common practice in the hospital for nurses to discontinue IV's without the order of a doctor. Is that correct?

   A. I would say it's a common practice for a nurse to discontinue IV when it's subcutaneous. . . .

. . . .

   Q. So anytime a patient should be so unfortunate to have his IV discontinued, pulls it out, something like that, that is the end of the IV?

   A. I did not say totally discontinued. . . .

Questions

4. How do the examples illustrate the differences the prosecutor and defendant are making in the interpretation of the aspectual meanings of the verbs *arrived, came, looked,* and *discontinued?*

======= **Part IV** =======

Data

1. *Q.* Do you recall, as you approached the nurses station, whether or not there were any people standing there?

   A. I believe there were some people standing there.

2. *Q.* Did you then go in?

   A. I believe—my intention was, you know, with the bell—I saw this doctor enter the room, and I believe I followed Dr. G., along with other people.

3. Q. What was your job there?
   A. I believe I got the crash cart from Mr. B.'s room, and went back to the Coronary Care Unit. . . .
4. Q. But, then you wanted to go to ICU.
   A. Yes. I believe that when I was on—working as a nursing supervisor I got interested working in ICU because I met these people in ICU who were very friendly. . . .
5. Q. So, did you say you three times applied to get into ICU, then?
   A. I believe I did.
6. Q. Isn't it common knowledge that the pharmacy would have supplied one for you if you had requested it?
   A. Well, I believe in the afternoon the pharmacy is closed.

Questions

5. How does this NNS use the term "I believe"? What is its function and how does it relate to standard English use of the term?

6. What impression does the NNS's use of the term leave with the listener?

*7. What do the data in this problem suggest about the interpretation of NNS speech?

**8. What do the data suggest about the differences between intended and received messages? Why is this difference particularly relevant in NS/NNS interactions?

**9. Relate your answer in (8) to a legal/medical context or other specific-purpose context you may be familiar with.

SECTION 8

Methodology and Research Design

This section focuses on issues related to research design and to the collection, analysis, and interpretation of IL data. As such, the concepts are not unique to SLA research.

Native Languages: Mixed
Target Language: English
Background Information: Adult university students
Data Source: Free compositions

Data

1. I am an accountant in Accounting Department of National Iranian Oil Company in Abadan which is one of the south cities of Iran.
2. There is a tire hanging down from the roof served as their playground.
3. Today you can find rural people that they don't have education.
4. My problem was to find a place has at least a yard for my children.
5. I wanted them to practice Chinese conversation what they learned every day.
6. When I return I plan to do accounting and supervising which is my interest and hope.
7. And it's a lovely view which you can see it from the plane.
8. Libya is quite a big country in which my home town is the biggest city.
9. Their philosophy depends on their education which they still working for it, as I am doing right now.
10. You can also go to the restaurant where you can have a good meal at a quiet table near the window.
11. I saw a group of people waiting for us.
12. Next week you give me a list of machine parts required in this contest.

Questions

1. Identify the restrictive and nonrestrictive relative clauses in the L2 sentences above.

2. List the criteria you used for deciding whether a sentence contained a restrictive or a nonrestrictive relative clause.

3. Are the criteria you used the same as those you used for determining restrictive and nonrestrictive relative clauses in standard English?

4. What is the major problem of analysis inherent in these data?

*5. What implications are there from this problem for analyzing research results in second language acquisition?

PROBLEM 8.2

Background Information: Description of experiment

Data

The experimenter wanted to compare the effectiveness of explanation coupled with classroom drill over explanation followed by language laboratory work on the acquisition of correct pronunciation by second language learners. She chose to conduct the experiment during a 7-week term at the English Language School. Six pronunciation teachers were assigned to six classes of fifteen students each. Two classes were classified as beginning, two as intermediate, and two as advanced according to a placement test consisting of listening comprehension, reading comprehension and grammar. The experimenter asked one teacher at each of the three levels to conduct the pronunciation class using explanation along with a period of language lab work, where each student was able to listen to a tape recorded model, record an imitation of the model, and play both the model and the imitation back for comparison. Students were given a paragraph to read at the beginning of the seven week term and at the end. Each teacher scored his/her students' pronunciation. At the end of the seven weeks, the experimenter collected both sets of scores and compared them. She found that the teachers conducting in-class drill sessions produced students with relatively fewer pronunciation problems at the end of the session. She therefore concluded that classroom drill is superior to language lab practice for the development of correct pronunciation in second language learners.

Questions

1. What flaws are there in the research design? That is, what did the researcher not control for which might reasonably be important to the interpretation of the results?

2. What other factors were not controlled for which may be unimportant or irrelevant to the interpretation of the results?

3. What other factors could the results be attributable to?

4. What specific aspects of the experiment are not clear from the description?

5. Is the researcher justified in making the claims she did regarding the acquisition of correct pronunciation? Why or why not?

PROBLEM 8.3

Native Language: German
Target Language: English
Background Information: Adult
Data Source: Composition and discussion about it

════ Part I ════

Data

But in that very moment it was six o'clock.

Questions

1. What aspect of grammar do you think this student is having difficulty with?

════ Part II ════

Data

After writing the sentence, the student maintained that it was correct, despite the fact that the teacher had offered the correct alternative by replacing *in* with *at*. The following conversation took place:

Teacher: Now you thought you were 100% right. I wrote "at that very moment." You are quite convinced that it is "in that very moment"?

Student: The only question would be, is it correct to say "it *was* six o'clock" or "It *had been* six o'clock"? That would be the only question.

Questions

2. Based on the student's comments, what do you think this student is really having difficulty with?

3. What does this example suggest about the relationship between difficulty and error?

PROBLEM 8.4

Native Language: English
Target Language: Spanish
Background Information: Adult university students
Data Source: Translation task, picture description, free composition

Data

Translation task scores

Category	Error %	Number of errors
		(in obligatory contexts)
Verb	5.4	61
Preposition	40.2	47
Pronoun	16.1	43
Adjective	3.6	5
Determiner	1.3	3

Picture description scores

Category	Error %	Number of errors
		(in obligatory contexts)
Verb	8.8	77
Preposition	28.0	67
Pronoun	15.7	20
Adjective	11.0	12
Determiner	4.1	42

Free composition scores

Category	Error %	Number of errors
		(in obligatory contexts)
Verb	11.2	108
Preposition	12.1	43
Pronoun	12.5	21
Adjective	13.5	38
Determiner	8.7	48

Questions

1. For each of the five grammatical categories examined, are the error rates similar across task type?

2. How do you account for the result in question 1?

*3. What general conclusion(s) can you draw from these data regarding the interpretation of L2 research results based on data from different tasks?

PROBLEM 8.5

Native Language: Arabic
Target Language: English
Background Information: Four adult ESL students
Data Source: Part I, grammaticality judgment and correction; Part II, interview; Part III, narrative

══════ Part I ══════

Data[1]

Subject 1

   1.   *She took the picture and put on the bulletin board.
                      put it on
   2.   *I won't know what is in the package until I receive.
                      I will receive it
   3.   *He took the ball and threw to Tom.
                      threw it

Subject 2

   1.   *She took the picture and put it on the bulletin board.
                      it
   2.   I won't know what is in the package until I receive.
   3.   He took the ball and threw to Tom.

Subject 3

   1.   She took the picture and put on the bulletin board.
   2.   I won't know what is in the package until I receive.
   3.   *He took the ball and threw to Tom.
                      it

Subject 4

   1.   She took the picture and put on the bulletin board.
   2.   *I won't know what is in the package until I receive.
                      I receive it
   3.   *He took the ball and threw to Tom.
                      threw it to

Questions

1. Based on the sentences in Part I, how would you characterize each learner's knowledge of direct object pronouns?

2. Which learner appears to be the most advanced in terms of direct object pronoun usage and why?

---

[1]In the data in Part I, * signifies that it was judged ungrammatical by the learner. The words in boldface under the sentences were the corrections made by the learner. Those sentences for which there is no * were judged grammatical.

====== **Part II** ======

Data[1]

Subject 1

  1. *I:* So no one has been treating it up to now.
     S: No, we can treat, can treat
  2. *S:* So that's the — major problem. But we can treat — we can use — one uh one drug —
  3. *S:* The problem is to know how to prevent it —
  4. *S:* Yeah, I know, because I — I discuss it with uh —the team leader of the project.

Subject 2

  1. I hope to take the best of the technical of the American (have) here. And then I used it when I return back.
  2. [šarbon] — we use it uh — in the heat — to to — in the house and uh — when you haven't electricity I can use wood — or uh — heat — or uh another object I don't know which ( ) It's a plant — we have uh — we can use uh — and now we we try to work on solar solar energy.

Subject 3

  1. But — I can ask him about the material which he is — lecture about — like physics chemis I can ask him about that — but anything else to translate or to — make again — because I — didn't get it — I can't make it.
  2. it's in my su — summer holiday you can say — I said why I don't use it — to be useful for me — to study here for two months — to live it and I heard about — University of Minnesota
  3. I was uh kind of afraid from America. I — I can't say that I don't like it but I didn't see it before that's the first time I come
  4. I have to show I prepare to study here because I found — they may agree they may not I am not sure about it — I'll try it when I return
  5. *I:* When you finish studying what do you hope to do then? What kind of things —
     S: When I — when I will do it?
  6. I don't know maybe here you count the labs —within the credits but in our country they don't — they don't uh — count it then it's about 156.

Subject 4

  1. *I:* . . . you have to know a lot about computers too? Or — not?
     S: As to how to use it —
  2. *I:* How to use it — What happens if the computer breaks down?
     S: . . . Change it.

Questions

  3. The above data were gathered in interviews with the subjects. They were told at the beginning of the interview to be careful to be grammatically correct, since their speech would later be judged for correctness. How would you characterize each learner's knowledge of direct object pronouns?

  4. Based on the data in Part II, which learner appears to be the most advanced?

Part III

Data

The following utterances are extracted from narratives elicited from these subjects.

Subject 1

1. and he took — one magazine or one magazine from the teacher's desk, and write it — uh and uh want to — to saw some pictures — and he put it in his in his desk, the student put the magazine in his desk.
2. he want he wants the magazine and he he didn't find it.

Subject 2

1. — the books of the teacher, that the h — the first student — has taken before — and she begin to look it — to look uh uh at the book
2. She begin to look at it and the — she put it not on the table of the teacher but she put it on her chair
3. the book — then — she put it — on the suitcase of the — of the — student — and — the — the first student come back and take her — suitcase and put it down

Subject 3

1. Then another girl — got the eraser and she (go) to the — board to erase it.
2. She found her — try to erase it and she said you did it — you did it. She said no I didn't do it and —

Subject 4

1. ... another — student — come — came in the — in the class and take the — the magazine — and put it — in the fir — in the first — student — bag

Questions

5. Based on the data in Part III, how would you characterize each learner's knowledge of direct object pronoun usage? (In Part III no instructions prior to the narration were given as to the necessity of being grammatically correct.)

6. In what way to the three elicitation situations of Parts I, II, and II differ?

7. If you were to learn that the subjects in each of the three elicitation situations were the same, how would you account for the different results?

8. What methodological issues does the information in question 7 suggest for the collection and interpretation of L2 acquisition results?

PROBLEM 8.6

Native Languages: Spanish (excerpts 1 to 6), French (excerpt 7)
Target Language: English
Background Information: 2 NNSs and 2 NSs. 2 NNSs residing in the United States from 2 to 4 years
Data Source: Description of objects or pictures (excerpts 1 to 6); spontaneous utterance (excerpt 7)

===== Part I =====

Data

1.   *NS:*   Does it make a noise?
     NNS: Noise (softly)
     NS: Noise (softly)
     NNS: No . . . No (softly)
     NS: No. uhm, is it sharp?
2.   *NS:*   No. uhm, is it sharp?
     NNS: sharp? no
     NS: is it uhm, . . . is it smooth?
     NNS: /smu/
     NS: smooth (gestures)
     NNS: yes
3.   *NS:*   hm, is it, uhm, is it made out of metal?
     NNS: metal, . . . no
4.   *NS:*   Okay, uhm, . . . you, uhm . . . when you eat you use it.
     NNS: uh . . . hm . . . spoon?
     NS: No . . . close!
     NNS: close.
     NS: What else do you eat with?
     NNS: Yes, but I don't know
     NS: Ah!
     NNS: the name
     NS: when you cut.
     NNS: yes, but I don't know the name (laughs)
     NS: (laughs)
     NNS: Yes!
     NS: you don't know the name?
     NNS: no
     NS: OK . . . you give up?
     NNS: yes
     NS: OK . . . it's a knife.
     NNS: the knife
5.   *NS:*   yeah! . . . yeah! you can . . . ask me like, for an idea, you know, to make it more easy.
     NNS: uh huh
     NS: So, go ahead. say, "What's it for?" You ask me, "What's it for?"
     NNS: What this for?
6.   *NS:*   Okay, little guy! yeah, yours! Okay! yours is it for eat?
     NNS: Eat. no.
7.   *NS:*   When I get to Paris, I'm going to sleep for one whole day. I'm so tired.
     NNS: What?
     NS: I'm going to sleep for one whole day.
     NNS: One hour a day?
     NS: Yes
     NNS: Why?
     NS: Because I'm so tired

Questions

1. In excerpts 1 to 6, what evidence is there that comprehension has taken place?

2. In excerpt 7, the conversation appears to flow like any normal conversation. Do you think these two participants have understood one another? Why or why not?

3. In excerpt 7, what is it that "allows" the conversation to proceed normally?

====== Part II ======

Data

Retrospective comments on the conversation (in Part I) by the participants (excerpts 1 to 6 only)

1. *NNS:* Noise—that I didn't understand.
   RES:[1] Why did you say "no" if you didn't understand the word?
   NNS: Because I thought she wouldn't be able to explain. There are some words—it's rare that a person can explain them.
   NS: I didn't think she understood "noise."
   RES: Why do you think she said "no" then?
   NS: Just to be safe. But I really don't think she understood.
   RES: Why didn't you pursue it then?
   NS: Hmm. I don't know.
2. *NNS:* "sharp" means "touched"
   NNS (after RES explains meaning): I should have listened in a different way.
   NNS: (re: smooth) something soft and "shaggy"
   NS: I did an audio-visual thing.
3. *NNS:* I didn't understand it, "metal"
   NS: I thought she understood it (metal).
4. *NNS:* I understood "clothes." I thought she meant something made of cloth. So, I was thinking of "tablecloth" and I didn't know how to say it.
   NS: (re: "close") I think because I gave her a positive response, she knew it was nearer to the right answer. But the word I'm not sure she understood.
   NNS: I was thinking of "tablecloth," but I didn't know the word in English.
   NNS: (re: cut). Like if I had "captured" what she said; if I was sure.
   NS: I just thought she couldn't think of the word. She knew it was a knife, but couldn't think of it.
   NNS: (re: give up) I wasn't real sure of the whole sentence, but, yes, I knew what she meant. There are some things it's not necessary to know real well. You understand from all the words together. I supposed she was telling me this—she'd take the thing out of the bag and I'd tell her it.

[1]RES = researcher.

168

RES: When she showed you the knife, what did you think?

NNS: I could never guess what that was what it was.

RES: Did you know how to say "knife" in English?

NNS: Yes

5. NNS: I understood "you ask me," but not "idea"

RES: Did you understand all that—to make it more easy for you?

NNS: No, I didn't understand it.

NNS: He (the NS) told me to tell him what I had. He said to me "What is it that you have?"

NS: Well, he just didn't have the language or know what to ask—on anything, he had no idea what to ask. So—I also forgot he could ask for what it's for a clue about it, so I just said, "Ask me what it's for and then I'll tell you."

RES: So he asked you what it's for. Do you think he understood then?

NS: Yes

6. RES: Did you understand the word "eat" this time?

NNS: "For eat." No, I didn't understand it.

Questions

4. Given these retrospection data, what conclusions can you draw about "appropriate responses" in conversations as indicators of comprehension?

*5. What do these data suggest about nonnative behavior in interactions with native speakers?

PROBLEM 8.7

Native Languages: Arabic, Farsi, Portuguese, Italian, Thai
Target Language: English
Background Information: Adult ESL students
Data Source: Sentence combining

Part I

Data

IL sentences by Arabic, Farsi, and Chinese speakers
1. John kissed the girl that her father was sick.
2. He saw the cat that jumped.
3. He saw the woman that the man gave her a flower.

IL sentence by Arabic and Farsi speakers
4. He saw the woman that the man kissed her.

IL sentence by Arabic speakers
5. He saw the woman that the man is older than her.

Information about Arabic, Farsi, and Chinese: All these languages have pronominal copies in relative clauses, but the languages differ in the relative clause types which have pronominal copies. Arabic has pronominal copies in direct object, indirect object, object of comparative and genitive positions. Farsi has the same distribution as Arabic with the exception of object of comparatives. Chinese has pronominal copies in indirect object, object of preposition, and genitives.

Questions

1. How would you describe the IL patterns in Part I?

2. Based on these data, how would you argue for or against the use of NL information in the acquisition of L2 relative clauses?

Part II

Data

IL sentences of Portuguese, Italian, and Thai speakers
1. The piano that the organ is bigger than it cost $800.
2. The boy which his girlfriend left fell down.
3. John kicked the ball that was rolling.
4. The boy gave a book to the girl that I saw.
5. I saw the girl whom the boy gave a book to.

Information about Portuguese, Italian, and Thai: These languages do not have pronominal copies in relative clauses.

3. What do the data in Part II suggest about language transfer?

4. Given the data in Parts I and II, what methodological considerations are necessary in order to argue for or against language transfer?

*5. How would you account for the use of pronominal copies in relative clauses by the L2 learners in this problem?

Native Language: Hebrew
Target Language: English
Background Information: 13- to 15-year-olds
Data Source: Elicited responses in interviews

Data

A. Israelis regularly produce sentences of the following type in their Hebrew-English IL:
1. I see him a year ago.
2. I saw the movie a couple of days ago.
3. I saw him in his apartment.
4. I study in school math science geography gym art.
5. I like English and geography best.
6. I like best Paul Anka Elvis Presley.
7. I live in Forest Park Apartments now.
8. I lived five years ago in Ramat Gan.

B. They do *not* produce sentences of the following type, where 1 is parallel to 1a, 2 to 2a, etc.:[1]
1a. *I see a year him ago.
2a. *I saw a couple of days the movie ago.
3a. *I saw in his him apartment.
4a. *I study math science in school geography gym art.
5a. *I like English best and geography.
6a. *I like Paul best Anka Elvis Presley.
7a. *I live in Forest now Park Apartments.
8a. *I lived five in Ramat Gan years ago.

Questions

1. Consider the concept "units of IL learning," in this case word order units that learners use in creating ILs. Looking at the linguistic material that occurs *after the verb* in the sentences of A, describe the word order unit which these learnerss are using in their IL.

2. How do the unattested forms in B provide evidence for a unit of IL word order?

Data

C. Sentences of the following NL-type, parallel to A, are attested for this IL:
1c. raiti   oto   lifney   šana.
     I saw   him before one year.
2c. raiti   et haseret   lifney   kama   yamin.
     I saw the movie   before several days.

---

[1] *indicates unattested forms.

3c. raiti   oto   badira   šelo.
   I saw   him   in his   apartment.

4c. ani   lomed   babet hasefer   matematika   madey hateva   geografia   hitamlut   omanut.
   I   study   in school   math   science   geography   gym   art.

5c. ani   ohev   meod   anglit   vegiografia.
   I   like   best   English   and geography.

   ani   meod   ohev   anglit   vegiografia.
   I   best   like   English   and geography.

6c. ani   ohev   meod   Paul Anka Elvis Presley.
   I   like   best   Paul Anka Elvis Presley.

   ani   meod   ohev   Paul Anka Elvis Presley.
   I   best   like   Paul Anka Elvis Presley.

7c. ani   gar   badirot   Forest Park   axšav.
   I   live   in   Forest Park Apartments   now.

   ani   gar   axšav   badirot   Forest Park.
   I   live   now   in   Forest Park Apartments.

8c. garti   lifney   xameš   šanim   beramat gan.
   I lived   before   five   years   in Ramat Gan.

   garti   beramat gan   lifney   xameš   šanim.
   I lived   in Ramat Gan   before   five   years.

D.   There are no parallel attested NL-type forms to B.

Questions

3. How does this NL evidence argue for or against the unit(s) you set up in questions 1 and 2?

4. Suppose that you were to learn that the transfer of *time-place* word order from the L1 (see sentences 7 and 8 above) is a widespread and persistent (i.e., fossilizable) phenomenon, being traced from Hebrew, German, Swedish, and Tagalog. How would this new information affect your concept of units of IL learning?

**5. Problem 4.9 and Appendix I provide more word order information on this IL. How do these additional data affect your concept of units of IL word order?

**6. Consider the restrictive/nonrestrictive information in Problem 8.1. How do these additional data affect your concept of units of IL learning?

Additional Data Sets

Problem 1.10

WEEK 1

Spontaneous utterances

Don't understand
Don't remember how you say it.
We don't know how automobile.
I don't understand.

I don't understand.
No remember.
I don't have time to go to college.

WEEK 3

Spontaneous utterances

I don't understand that.
I don't have much time.
I don't have the car.
I don't understand.
You don't understand me?
Don't know.
I don't remember.
I don't give nothing.
No like walk.
I no understand.
That "learn" no understand.
No remember.
No remember.
No understand that.

I no understand good.
I no understand.
I no understand this word.
No understand this.
I no understand this (rogation).
No have pronunciation.
Why isn't the girl . . .
No understand all.
No understand all.
No is mine.
I no may explain to you.
Because no gain for the year.
No pass.

WEEK 7

Spontaneous utterances

I don't remember.
No understand.
I no remember this name.
Yeah, no repeat this inversion, no?
No understand.
I no know.
I no understand.
I no understand.
I no understand this question.

I no understand that.
I no understand.
But no understand.
You after [=before] no talk nothing English.
I no can.
I no make, no can repeat the (oracion), no?
I don't can explain.
You no like Coca-cola?

Elicited data[1] (change sentences to negatives)

JOHN, COME AT FIVE O'CLOCK.
  John, don't come in five o'clock.
SIT DOWN THERE.
  No sit.
COME AT FIVE O'CLOCK.
  I no come.
THE BOY WANTS A COOKIE.
  He no eat cookie.
SHE WANTS SOME DINNER.
  She don't want some dinner.
HE WENT OUTSIDE.
  He no, not come outside.
THE GIRL ATE SOME SOUP.
  He not eat soup.

SHE SAW HIM.
  She don't saw him.
THE GIRL ASKED SOMEONE.
  She don't answer.
THE BABY IS CRYING.
  She is don't crying.
SOMEBODY IS COMING IN.
  They don't come in.
THE DOG CAN BARK.
  The dog don't can bark.
THE GLASS WILL BREAK.
  Glass, it does, don't break.

---

[1]The first sentence listed in capital letters is the stimulus, the second sentence is the response.

WEEK 11

Spontaneous utterances

I don't /espeak/ English.
I don't talk English.
I don't talk.
I don't understand this name.
I don't ask this.
I no like my coffee.
No like coffee.
Friday, Saturday and Sunday I no take nothing.
I no understand this conversation.
No remember.

I no remember.
I sometimes no understand.
No understand that.
(Yo) [=I] no remember.
No is good here?
Sky no is this.
I don't can more.
I no can explain this.
You no will come here this vacation?

Elicited data[1] (change sentence to negative)

I WANT SOME PAPER.
   You don't want some (people).
COME BACK TOMORROW.
   I don't come back tomorrow.
WHY DO WE GO TO SCHOOL?
   I don't go to school.
YOU REMEMBER.
   I don't remember.
YOU TALK VERY MUCH.
   I don't talk too much.
I NEED TO TALK TO YOU.
   I don't need to talk to you.
YOU LIKE COCA-COLA.
   I don't like this is Coca-cola.
I ASK THIS QUESTION.
   I don't ask this question.
I WALK.
   I don't walk.
THE TEACHER LIKES THE STUDENT.
   She don't like students.
THE GIRL PLAYS VOLLEYBALL.
   Don't like playing volleyball.
HE WATCHES T.V.
   He don't watch T.V.
SHE TOLD HIM TO OPEN IT.
   She /dud/ not /dost/ that, /dos/, /dos/.
THEY RODE THE BUS.
   I don't take . . . the bus.

MR. S. ASKED EVERYBODY.
   He don't ask nothings.
THE BOYS PLAYED SOME CHESS.
   They do not play (e) xxx chess.
HE SAID TO ME.
   He don't send to me.
THIS IS A TABLE.
   Do not is a table.
HE IS A STUDENT.
   He's don't (tua) student.
THIS IS MY PROBLEM.
   That no is my problem.
I AM STRONG.
   I don't strong.
I WAS A BARTENDER.
   I am not (asa) bartender.
SOMEBODY IS SINGING.
   They don't sing.
THEY ARE PAINTING THE HOUSE.
   They don't painting the house.
THE DOG CAN BARK.
   He do not come.
THE BOYS CAN RIDE BICYCLES.
   They do not come bicycles.
THE BUS WILL BE HERE AT TWO-THIRTY.
   It don't come two-thirty.

WEEK 17

Spontaneous utterances

I don't pay.
I don't understand.
I don't have a woman.
I no remember.
No work in my factory.
No talk English here.
I no remember.
I no remember.
I no remember.
I no understand good.
Maybe these no have education.
In my country no haves too much friends.
No like.
No like eat.

No remember.
No like more, thank you.
This no have calendar.
No have special shoes.
We no walk for the center.
No look his name.
No say nothing me.
The people no pay tax.
Any times no talk nothing.
Sometime no talk to you.
No talk to him.
No say nothing.
No is subject.
No is /constitutional/.

WEEK 21

Spontaneous utterances

The people no have money.
You no go is come here police.
Maybe no like this state.

You ([=they]) don't speak Spanish?
Daughters no take this illness.
No have holidays.

---

[1]The first sentence listed in capital letters is the stimulus, the second sentence is the response.

I no like this summer.
No see more.
No remember this name.
She no go more.
He no sleep.
No drink too much.
No take my books.
I no speak nothing English.
I no have friend.
I no have application.
No have nothing.
No is good.
No is cassette, is tape.
No is problem.
I no can walk.
You don't have religion.
I don't speak English.

I no have holidays.
No eat meat.
I no remember.
No remember.
I no have money.
You no like these cigarettes.
I no remember this mark of cigarettes.
She no has other brother.
I don't saw.
George no is my brother.
No make cut.
I don't can let this job.
People don't can pass the jungle.
Columbia don't can make.
No can make nothing.
No put sick.
Maybe she no live more.

WEEK 33

Spontaneous utterances

I don't understand this question.
I don't remember this name.
Why you no smoke?
No read.
I no speak English very nice, no?
I no remember this name.
I no remember the name.
I no remember.
No speak English, yeah?

He no make nothing job in this picture.
He no work because all the time he estudent.
I don't saw.
This isn't a supper, is a lunch.
No is good place.
No is good?
I don't can read, write English.
I don't can make that.
If I talk English very nice, he no say that me.

Elicited data[1] (change sentence to negative)

SOMETIMES HE PLAYS POOL.
    You no did play pool.
SOMETIMES SHE PLAYS POOL.
    You no play the pool.
HE LIKES EVERYBODY.
    You no like anybody.

HE LIKES EVERYBODY.
    You do no like or you no like everybody.
HE HAS SOME MONEY.
    He don't haves any money.
I WENT SOMEWHERE.
    You don't go somewhere.

WEEK 35

Spontaneous utterances

I don't care.
I don't understand.
I don't understand that.
I don't care.
No repeat.
No have sister.

I no eat nothing.
No drink nothing.
No understand.
I don't can explain.
I don't can explain this picture.

Elicited data[1] (change sentence to negative)

BOTH OF THEM WANT SUPPER.
    These people don't like supper.
HE GOES TO SCHOOL.
    He don't go to school.
SHE LIKES POTATO CHIPS AND HE DOES, TOO.
    She don't like the potato chips. And he('d) don't like that.
HE RIDES BICYCLES JUST LIKE SHE DOES.
    He don't ride the bicycle.
HE WANTED COFFEE FOR BREAKFAST.
    He don't want coffee to the breakfast.
HE PLAYED WITH SOME BALLS.
    He don't played with, don't balls.
THEY SAID IT WAS RAINING.
    They don't say/sell, it's/is raining.
SOMEBODY THREW IT AWAY.
    Somebody don't threw it away.
THIS IS A CHAIR.
    That no is chair.

THE BOY IS TALL.
    He don't /s/ tall.
SHE IS GOING TO THE STORE.
    She don't go to the store.
THEY ARE PLAYING BASEBALL.
    They are don't play basketball.
HE WAS TALKING TO THE TEACHER.
    He don't was talking the teacher.
ANYBODY CAN PLAY WITH IT.
    Anybody don't can't this (payed) it.
HE COULD TAKE A BUS.
    He don't like take a bus.
HE WILL DRINK HIS BEER.
    He don't will drink beer.
SHE'S GOT A NEW DRESS.
    She don't /cut/ [=got] the dress.
SHE HAS EATEN HER DINNER.
    She don't has eaten in the dinner.

---

[1]The first sentence listed in capital letters is the stimulus, the second sentence is the response.

Problem 4.6

Several different sentence types (resulting from learners' "sentence-producing tactics") are presented for one child over a 9-month period, divided into four time periods.

TIME I

Sentence type 1

My name is John.
I dunno.

How much?
Thank you.

Thank you very much.
Goodbye.

Sentence type 2

Papa
Father (=men)
Girl (=women, girls)
Boy

Mother
Sangwish (=anything edible)
Grandpa (=older men)
Doggy, dog (=cats and dogs)

House (=buildings)
Three girls
Four boys
Two fathers

(In sentence type 2, noun phrases are responses to questions.)

TIME II

Sentence type 1

I dunno.
Oh hi, Stupid!
You are stupid.
My name is John.
Shaddup you.
OK, OK, OK!
OK, sir!
Hey lookit, lookit!

What?
Gimme one, please!
C'mon!
Hey, what'a you name?
Goodbye!
Bye bye!
What is this?

Nothing!
Hello.
Wha'sa matter?
Come here.
Come.
Come in.
One more.

Sentence type 2

I wanna be the doctor.

I wanna be the cowbody.

Sentence type 3

The car
The big blocks
Five minutes

Two cars
Girl
Boy

Monkey
Dog

(In sentence type 3, the utterances are mostly responses to questions.)

TIME III

Sentence type 1

Oh, Teacher.
Look Teacher.
Hey, Carlos.

No, Kevin!
OK, Teacher.
My turn, Kevin.

I can't, Teacher.
One more, Teacher.

Sentence type 2

What is it?
Where am I?
Oh yeah?
Oh, [name].
Look!

Hey!
Oh boy.
Here.
I dunno.

I can't.
Wait, wait, wait.
Wait a minute.
C'mon.

Sentence type 3

Your turn

My turn

One more (three more, etc.)

Sentence type 4

Mine
You, I
My (=me)

Dese ("Dese, dese, dese!"
       "Dese and dese and dese")

Sentence type 5

Four apples
Three ball

Two boys
One car

One boy
Three mine

Sentence type 6

The cars
Monkey
Dog

Animal
An boy
The peanuts

Elephant
The little cookies
The yellow car

Sentence type 7

Es my.	Here dog.	It's your turn.
Es da applay. (="apple")	Here my.	This is elephant.
Es da elephant.	Here one more.	Who has the peanuts?
It mine.	Hey one car.	Who has four balls?
We got an boy.	It my turn.	Who has the car?
We got one more.	This is your turn, your turn.	

Sentence type 8

I finish.	I do. You do. (Answer to question,	I stand up.
You finish.	"Who has the X?")	You stand up.

TIME IV

Sentence type 1

My turn, teacher.	OK, Teacher!	Get it, Carlos.
That mine, Carlos?		

Sentence type 2

Ready, get set, go!	Hey, look!	Yikes!
Look!	Stopit!	Get it!
What's this?	My name is John.	I dunno.

Sentence type 3

My turn	Your turn	One more

Sentence type 4

Me (="I")	Dese	He
You	It	She (="He, she")
Mine		

Sentence type 5

Three turns	Four marble	Two twenties
Two red		

Sentence type 6

The book	A Indians	[Number]
The door	A car	

Sentence type 7

Your turn and my turn	Two twenties and one thirty	One more and one more

Sentence type 8

Right here	Here	Fast
Like this	In here	

Sentence type 9

Close the door.	Me got right here.	Go the door. (="Go to the door.")
Sit down right here.	He got like this.	Go the chair, the big chair. (="Go to
Sit down in here.	Carlos got here.	the chair.")
Read the book.	You got thirty?	Go the book. (="Bring me the book.")
I got twenty.	Me got three turns.	Throw the box.
Me got twenty.	Me got it right here, too!	Throw it right here.
You got right here.		

Sentence type 10

Your turn and my turn!	The book!	My turn!
Your turn!	One more!	Dese!
Three turn.	A Indians!	

Problem 4.9

1. Where are the books now?

The books are now in your hand.
The books are in your hand now.
The books the books are in your hands.
Now the books are in your hand.

The books now are in your hand.
The books are now on the table.
The book is on the table.

2. Where did I put the books?

You put the book in the desk.
You put the books on the the on the chair.
You put the books on the table now.
You put the books on the table.

You put the books on the table.
You put the book the books on the table.
The books are on the table.

3. What subjects do you study in school?

I learn geography mathematic mathematic.
I study in school mathematics history geography.
I study at school mathematics Hebrew.
In school I I learn English Hebrew.

I studied at school historia mathematica and sport.
I'm study in school the same subjects.
We learn we learn in school Hebrew mathematics science.

4. What subject do you like best?

I like the mathematics.
I like best history.
I like best the the geo— Hebrew lessons.
I like best geography history and Hebrew.

I like mathematics best.
Best I like English and ma— mathematics.
I like best mathematics.

5. When did you meet your teacher?

I met Mr. Yanko two years ago.
I meet Nomi three three years ago.
I met him three years ago.
I met Mr. Margaliot two years ago.

I met her at the beginning of the year.
I met her a year before.
I met my mathematics teacher before two years.

6. Where did you buy that watch?

I got it for a present.
I bought my watch in the town.
I buy my watch in the shop.
I get it from America.

I bought it in Haifa.
I bought my watch in Tel Aviv.
My father bought it.

7. When did you buy it?

I bought this watch before one year.
I get it before five year.
I I get the watch when I was 12 year.
I buy it three years ago.

I bought my watch two years ago.
I bought it three three years ago.
My father bought it six or seven years ago.

8. Do you like movies?

Yes I like them very much.
Yes I like very much movies.
I like movies very much.
I like it very much.

Yes I like movies.
Yes sure I like very much movies.
I like very much films.

9. What type of movie do you like best?

Best I like movies about gangsters war.
I like funny movies.
I love movies of famous men.
I like to see cowboys movies.

I like best the Tarzan.
I like best the the history movies.
I like comic movies and some serious ones.

10. When did you see that movie?

I saw My Fair Lady last week.
I see it yesterday.
Yesterday I saw America America.
I saw it two days two days ago.

I see the movie a few days ago.
I saw this film last week.
I saw it before two months.

11. Where do you live now?

I live now at 61 Rambam Street.
Now I live in Jerusalem.
I live in Jerusalem.
I live now in Jerusalem.

Now I'm living in Tel Aviv.
I live now in Ramat Gan.
Now I also live in Ramat Gan.

12. Where did you live five years ago?

I lived five years ago in Ramat Gan.
I lived in Tel Aviv.
I live in Jerusalem five years ago.
I li— I I lived in Aliya Street.

I li— I I lived also in Ramat Gan.
Five years ago I lived in Ramat Gan.
I I have been living in Lud.

13. What singer do you like best?

The Israel singer I like best is Rivka Michaeli.
The best I like the singer Elvis Presley.
I like best the Beatles.
I like Nehama Hendel best.

I like be— the best Nehama Hendel.
I like Be— Benny Berman the best.
I like best Paul Anka Elvis Presley.

14. When did you hear that singer?
I I hear Rivka Michaeli yesterday.
I hear them ye— yesterday.
I heard them always in the radio.
I heard her last yesterday.

Yesterday I heard the the Beatles.
One year ago I have I have heard her.
I think yesterday I have heard her.

15. When did you see your doctor?
I saw Dr. Halevi last year.
I saw Dr. Drifus before one year.
I saw him eight years ago.
I see Dr. Sneh two months ago.

I saw her the last time two months ago.
I see him a year ago.
I saw him last before two month.

16. Where did you see him?
I see Mr. Lavon in Ben Yehuda Street.
I saw him in his room.
I saw him in my house.
I saw him in his in his apartment.

I saw him in his office.
I saw him in his house.
In Ramat Gan I saw him.

17. What will you study in the university? What will you study there?
I want to study biologia.
I will study there languages.
I I want to study in the university law.
I will study to be lawyer.

I will study languages there.
I will learn there English and French.
I want to study in the university chemistry and biochemistry.

APPENDIX II
Sources

Section 1: Morphology

1.1 Janusz Arabski (1979); **1.2** Sandra Deline, Patricia Jensen, and Asma Omar (original data); **1.3** Bruno Sauzier (1979); **1.4** Edith Hanania (1974); **1.5** Benji Wald (original data); **1.6** Edith Hanania (1974); **1.7** Sandra Deline, Patricia Jensen, and Asma Omar (original data); **1.8** Elaine Tarone, Uli Frauenfelder, and Larry Selinker (1976); **1.9** Benji Wald (original data); **1.10** John Schumann (1978)

Section 2: Lexicon

2.1 Josh Ard and Susan Gass (original data); **2.2** Larry Selinker, Merrill Swain, and Guy Dumas (1975) and Elaine Tarone, Uli Frauenfelder, and Larry Selinker (1976); **2.3** Sandra Deline, Patricia Jensen, and Asma Omar (original data); **2.4** Larry Selinker, Merrill Swain, and Guy Dumas (1975) and Elaine Tarone, Uli Frauenfelder, and Larry Selinker (1976); **2.5** Larry Selinker, Merrill Swain, and Guy Dumas (1975) and Elaine Tarone, Uli Frauenfelder, and Larry Selinker (1976); **2.6** Christian Adjemian (1983); **2.7** Eric Kellerman (1979); **2.8** Shoshana Blum and E. A. Levenston (1979)

Section 3: Phonology

3.1 Ellen Broselow (1983); **3.2** Fred Eckman (1981); **3.3** Fred Eckman (1981); **3.4** Lonna and Wayne Dickerson (1977); **3.5** Elaine Tarone (1980); **3.6** A. A. Darbeeva (1976a, b, and c). Data organized by Josh Ard; **3.7** Leslie Beebe (1980)

Section 4: Syntax/Semantics

4.1 Sandra Deline, Patricia Jensen, and Asma Omar (original data); **4.2** Masayuki Kishi and Dennis Preston (1984); **4.3** Susan Gass (original data); **4.4** Kenji Hakuta (1974); **4.5** Sandra Deline, Patricia Jensen, and Asma Omar (original data); **4.6** Lily Wong-Fillmore (1976); **4.7** Susan Gass and Josh Ard (1984); **4.8** Roger Andersen (1983); **4.9** Larry Selinker (1966, 1969)

Section 5: Spoken and Written Discourse

5.1 Charlotte Basham, Joe Mattingly, and Karen Tucker Al-Batal (original data); **5.2** Charlotte Basham, Joe Mattingly, and Karen Tucker Al-Batal (original data); **5.3** Guillermo Bartelt (1983); **5.4** Moira Chimombo (original data); **5.5** Moira Chimombo (original data); **5.6** Garifullina (1976) as cited in E. M. Axunzjanov (1978). Data organized by Josh Ard; **5.7** Birgit Harley (1982); **5.8** Elite Olshtain (1983)

Section 6: Foreigner Talk Discourse

6.1 Michael Long (1983); **6.2** Evangeline Varonis and Susan Gass (1982); **6.3** Patricia Porter (1983); **6.4** Ann E. Chun, Richard R. Day, N. Ann Chenoweth, Stuart Luppescu (1982); **6.5** Robin Scarcella (1983); **6.6** Evangeline Varonis and Susan Gass (1984); **6.7** Evangeline Varonis and Susan Gass (1982) and Susan Gass (original data); **6.8** JoAnne Kleifgen (in press)

Section 7: Specific-Purpose Acquisition

7.1 Larry Selinker and Dan Douglas (original data); **7.2** Larry Selinker and Dan Douglas (in preparation); **7.3** Larry Selinker and Dan Douglas (in preparation); **7.4** Larry Selinker (original data); **7.5** Patricia Rounds (original data); **7.6** Paz Naylor (unpublished ms.)

Section 8: Methodology and Research Design

8.1 Jacquelyn Schachter (original data); **8.2** Hypothetical situation proposed by Jan Smith; **8.3** Eric Kellerman (1974); **8.4** Veronica LoCoco (1976); **8.5** Elaine Tarone (1983); **8.6** Barbara Hawkins (in press) and Susan Gass (original data); **8.7** Susan Gass (1979a and b); **8.8** Larry Selinker (1966, 1969)

Appendix I

Problem 1.10 John Schumann (1978); **Problem 4.6** Lily Wong-Fillmore (1976); **Problem 4.9** Larry Selinker (1966)

APPENDIX III

Index of Interlanguages

Native languages are listed first; e.g., French-English refers to French as the L1 and English as the L2

IL	*Problem Number*
Apache-English	5.3
Arabic-English	1.2, 1.4, 1.6, 1.7, 2.3, 3.1, 4.1, 4.5, 5.1, 6.8, 8.5, 8.7
Buryat-Russian	3.6
Cantonese-English	3.5
Chichewa-English	5.4, 5.5
Dutch-English	2.7
English-French	1.8, 2.2, 2.4, 2.5, 2.6, 5.7
English-Hebrew	2.8, 5.8
English-Spanish	4.8, 8.4
Farsi-English	8.7
French-English	2.6, 8.6
German-English	7.5, 8.3
Hebrew-English	4.9, 8.8
Hungarian-Hebrew	2.8
Italian-English	5.2, 8.7
Japanese-English	3.4, 4.2, 4.3, 4.4, 4.7, 6.6, 6.8
Korean-English	3.5, 6.8
Mandarin-English	3.3, 7.4
Navajo-English	5.3
Polish-English	1.1
Portuguese-English	3.5, 8.7
Rumanian-Hebrew	2.8
Russian-Hebrew	5.8
Spanish-English	1.3, 1.5, 1.9, 1.10, 3.2, 4.6, 4.7, 6.3, 6.5, 6.6, 7.1, 7.2, 7.3, 7.5, 8.6
Spanish-Hebrew	2.8
Tagalog-English	7.6
Tatar-Russian	5.6
Thai-English	3.7, 8.7
Urdu-English	6.8

REFERENCES

Adjemian, C. 1983. The transferability of lexical properties. In S. Gass and L. Selinker (eds.) *Language Transfer in Language Learning.* Rowley, Mass.: Newbury House.

Andersen, R. 1983. Transfer to somewhere. In S. Gass and L. Selinker (eds.) *Language Transfer in Language Learning.* Rowley, Mass.: Newbury House.

Arabski, J. 1979. *Errors as Indications of the Development of Interlanguage.* Kotowice: Uniwersytet Slaski.

Axunzjanov, E. M. 1978. O razgranicenii interferencii i transferencii v uslovijax jazykovyx kontaktov. *Voprosy jazykoznanija.* 5. 72–81.

Bartelt, H. G. 1983. Transfer and variability of rhetorical redundancy in Apachean English inter-language. In S. Gass and L. Selinker (eds.) *Language Transfer in Language Learning.* Rowley, Mass.: Newbury House.

Beebe, L. 1980. Sociolinguistic variation and style shifting in second language acquisition. *Language Learning.* 30.2. 433–448.

Blum, S., and E. A. Levenston. 1979. Lexical simplification in second language acquisition. *Studies in Second Language Acquisition.* 2.2. 43–64.

Broselow, E. 1983. Nonobvious transfer: on predicting epenthesis errors. In S. Gass and L. Selinker (eds.) *Language Transfer in Language Learning.* Rowley, Mass.: Newbury House.

Chun, N., R. Day, N. A. Chenoweth, and S. Luppescu. 1982. Types of errors corrected in native-nonnative conversations. *TESOL Quarterly.* 16.2. 537–547.

Darbeeva, A. 1976a. Sravnitel'naja xarakteristika osnovnyx strukturnyx osobennostej burjatskogo i russkogo jazykov. In J. D. Deseriev (ed.) *Razvitie Nacional'no-russkogo Dvujazycija.* Moscow: Nauka.

Darbeeva, A. 1976b. Pervaja stupen' burjatsko-russkogo dvujazycija. In J. D. Deseriev (ed.) *Razvitie Nacional'no-russkogo Dvujazycija.* Moscow: Nauka.

Darbeeva, A. 1976c. Vtoraja stupen' burjatsko-russkogo dvujazycija. In J. D. Deseriev (ed.) *Razvitie Nacional'no-russkogo Dvujazycija.* Moscow: Nauka.

Dickerson, W., and L. Dickerson. 1977. Interlanguage phonology: current research and future directions. In S. P. Corder and E. Roulet (eds.) *Actes du 5ème Colloque de Linguistique Appliquée de Neuchatel.* Genève: Librairie Droz.

Eckman, F. 1981. On the naturalness of interlanguage phonological rules. *Language Learning.* 31. 1. 195–216.

Garifullina, M. 1976. Programmirovannoe obucenie russkomu jazyku v nacal'nyx klassax tatarskoj skoly. Candidate Dissertation. Kazan'.

Gass, S. 1979a. Language transfer and universal grammatical relations. *Language Learning.* 29.2. 327–344.

Gass, S. 1979b. An investigation of syntactic transfer in adult second language acquisition. Ph.D. Dissertation. Indiana University.

Gass, S., and J. Ard. 1984. L2 acquisition and the ontology of language universals. In W. Rutherford (ed.) *Second Language Acquisition and Language Universals.* Amsterdam: John Benjamins Press.

Gleason, H. 1955. *Workbook in Descriptive Linguistics.* New York: Holt, Rinehart and Winston.

Halle, M., and G. Clements. 1983. *Problem Workbook in Phonology.* Cambridge: MIT Press.

Hakuta, K. 1974. Prefabricated patterns and the emergence of structure in second language acquisition. *Language Learning.* 24. 2. 287–298.

Hanania, E. 1974. Acquisition of English structures: a case study of an adult native speaker of Arabic in an English-speaking environment. Ph.D. Dissertation. Indiana University.

Harley, B. 1982. Age-related differences in the acquisition of the French verb system by anglophone students in French immersion programs. Ph.D. Dissertation. University of Toronto.

Hawkins, B. In press. Is an "appropriate response" always so appropriate? In S. Gass and C. Madden. *Language Input in Second Language Acquisition.* Rowley, Mass.: Newbury House.

Kellerman, E. 1974. Elicitation, lateralisation and error analysis. *York Papers in Linguistics.* 4.

Kellerman, E. 1979. Transfer and nontransfer: where we are now. *Studies in Second Language Acquisition.* 2. 1. 37–59.

Kishi, M., and D. Preston. 1984. A good sentence to say: infinitive modifiers in English. *New Organon.*

Kleifgen, J. In press. Skilled variation in a kindergarten teacher's use of foreigner talk. In S. Gass and C. Madden. *Language Input in Second Language Acquisition.* Rowley, Mass.: Newbury House.

LoCoco, V. 1976. A comparison of three methods for the collection of L2 data: Free composition, translation, and picture description. *Working Papers on Bilingualism.* 8. 60–86.

Long, M. 1983. Linguistic and conversational adjustments to non-native speakers. *Studies in Second Language Acquisition.* 5. 2. 177–193.

Naylor, P. Unpublished ms. Legal testimony and the non-native speaker of English: the problem of linguistic and cultural interference in interethnic communication.

Nida, E. 1946. *Morphology.* Ann Arbor: University of Michigan Press.

Olshtain, E. 1983. Sociocultural competence and language transfer: the case of apology. In S. Gass and L. Selinker (eds.) *Language Transfer in Language Learning.* Rowley, Mass.: Newbury House.

Porter, P. 1983. How learners talk to each other: input and interaction in task-centered discussions. Paper presented at TESOL, Toronto.

Sauzier, B. 1979. Interlanguage/error analysis of a highly fossilized Mexican Spanish speaker. Unpublished ms. UCLA.

Scarcella, R. 1983. Discourse accent in second language performance. In S. Gass and L. Selinker (eds.) *Language Transfer in Language Learning.* Rowley, Mass.: Newbury House.

Schumann, J. 1978. *The Pidginization Process: A Model for Second Language Acquisition.* Rowley, Mass.: Newbury House.

Selinker, L. 1966. A psycholinguistic study of language transfer. Ph.D. Dissertation. Georgetown University.

Selinker, L. 1969. Language transfer. *General Linguistics.* 9. 67–92.

Selinker, L., and D. Douglas. In preparation. Wrestling with "context" in IL theory.

Selinker, L., M. Swain, and G. Dumas. 1975. The interlanguage hypothesis extended to children. *Language Learning.* 25. 139–152.

Tarone, E. 1980. Some influences on the syllable structure of interlanguage phonology. *IRAL.* 18.2. 139–152.

Tarone, E. 1983. Evidence of style-shifting in interlanguage use. Paper presented at AAAL, Minneapolis.

Tarone, E., U. Frauenfelder, and L. Selinker. 1976. Systematicity/variability and stability/instability in interlanguage systems. *Language Learning.* Special Issue 4. 93–134.

Varonis, E., and S. Gass. 1982. The comprehensibility of non-native speech. *Studies in Second Language Acquisition.* 4.2 114–136.

Varonis, E., and S. Gass. 1984. Non-native/non-native conversations: a model for negotiation of meaning. *Applied Linguistics.* 6. 1.

Wong-Fillmore, L. 1976. The second time around: cognitive and social strategies in second language acquisition. Ph.D. Dissertation. Stanford.